€ 16,50

D0862352

Napoleon's Guards of Honour

1813–14

Ronald Pawley • Illustrated by Patrice Courcelle

Series editor Martin Windrow

First published in Great Britain in 2002 by Osprey Publishing
Elms Court, Chapel Way, Botley, Oxford OX2 9LP, United Kingdom
Email: **info@ospreypublishing.com**

ISBN 1 84176 488 4
Editor: Martin Windrow
Design: Alan Hamp
Index by Alan Rutter

Originated by Magnet Harlequin, Uxbridge, UK.
Printed in China through World Print Ltd.

02 03 04 05 06   10 9 8 7 6 5 4 3 2 1

FOR A CATALOGUE OF ALL BOOKS PUBLISHED BY
OSPREY MILITARY AND AVIATION PLEASE CONTACT:
**The Marketing Manager, Osprey Direct UK, PO Box 140
Wellingborough, Northants, NN8 2FA, United Kingdom**
Email: **info@ospreydirect.co.uk**

**The Marketing Manager, Osprey Direct USA, c/o MBI Publishing
729 Prospect Avenue, Osceola, WI 54020, USA**
Email: **info@ospreydirectusa.com**

www.ospreypublishing.com

DE KRIJGER

Boekhandel &
Uitgeverij

Dorpsstraat 144 - B-9420 Erpe

Tel. (053) 80 84 49 - Fax (053) 80 84 53

Acknowledgements

Mrs Ilse Bogaerts, responsible for the textile department of the Royal Army Museum in Brussels, and the staff of the museum; and M. Alain Chappet for opening his pictorial collection of Napoleonic monuments.

Artist's Note

Readers may care to note that the original paintings from which the colour plates in this book were prepared are available for private sale. All reproduction copyright whatsoever is retained by the Publishers. All enquiries should be addressed to:

Patrice Courcelle, 33 avenue des Vallons, 1410 Waterloo, Belgium

The Publishers regret that they can enter into no correspondence upon this matter.

NAPOLEON'S GUARDS OF HONOUR
1813–14

NAPOLEON'S DILEMMA

I N LATE JUNE 1812, when Napoleon's Grande Armée crossed the River Niemen to invade Russia, it was probably the largest and strongest army that had ever been gathered for a single campaign throughout recorded history. They needed four days and three bridges to cross the Niemen. From the whole of Europe they came: from France, from what are now Holland and Belgium, from Spain, Portugal, Switzerland, Italy and the Balkans, and from every corner of Germany – even from defeated Austria and Prussia, which were obliged to send allied troops to advance on the outer flanks of the invading army. However, although some 400,000 strong, the ranks were no longer filled by the victors of Austerlitz.

Most of the veterans who had followed the eagles in 1805 had disappeared, paying the everlasting human tax of Bonaparte's continual wars – some were paying it still, in Spain, the 'ulcer' of the empire. The veterans who remained were mainly serving in the Imperial Guard. In 1812 the soldiers of the Line were the former conscripts who had fought at Friedland (1807) and Wagram (1809) – not the real old 'grumblers', perhaps, but still experienced, battle-proven regiments clad in striking uniforms and led by veteran commanders.

Six months later, only one bridge across the Niemen would suffice to carry home the returning shadow of the former Grande Armée; and if the few tens of thousands left crossed it slowly, it was because they were sick, footsore and starving. Near the Polish border, Napoleon, passing over command to his brother-in-law Murat, left the wretched tatters behind and headed directly for France, where he had somehow to rebuild an army. For the first time in his career a war had not ended with a single campaign, and gathering a new army would present him with many difficulties.

Most of Napoleon's immediately available remaining experienced troops were fighting the Duke of Wellington's Anglo-Portuguese army in Spain in defence of his brother's puppet throne, and he did not want to weaken this second front. Infantry was not the problem: young conscripts could be gathered in, and trained – more or less

Hand-coloured engraving by Martinet. The same engraving was used to represent each regiment; the only changes the artist had to make were the number on the sabretache and portmanteau, and the colour of the tip of the plume. (Collection of Belgian Royal Army Museum, Brussels)

3

– while marching to join the army in Germany; but the cavalry was different. Horses themselves were in short supply after the hecatomb of Russia; and horse soldiers had to be trained to ride and care for their beasts, and to master the manoeuvres needed in the field. Instructing the light cavalry to the point where they could serve efficiently was particularly difficult: they were the eyes of the army, on which it depended for scouting and screening, and their mission required officers and NCOs who could operate independently without constant supervision by senior commanders. It was believed that to train good light cavalrymen normally took as long as three years – and Bonaparte needed them in three months.

What Napoleon needed were educated men of private means, accustomed to riding, who could not only learn their trade quickly but also provide their own horses and pay for their own uniforms and equipment. For many years he had tried to attract the 'cream of society' throughout his empire into his military service. In 1807, for example, he had created the Gendarmes d'ordonnance, a mounted and foot corps consisting mainly of noblemen; in all some 394 would serve, but under pressure from his jealous Imperial Guard he was more or less obliged to disband them. (The attempt was not a total failure, as the Gendarmes d'ordonnance would provide his army with about ten generals and 24 colonels.)

Now, with a cavalry arm that had bled or frozen to death in the snows of Russia (or had simply drifted away from the line of march as soon as they reached safe territory), Napoleon decided that the situation obliged him to call upon the sons of the leading classes from all over the empire. This was not only a military necessity but also a political one. When he was sitting on his throne in Paris, he was still the most powerful man in Europe; but the disaster in Russia had made his position somewhat fragile, and the new 'Gardes d'honneur' would be considered in some sense as hostages, to ensure the continuing loyalty of those families who played a large part in the organisation and administration of the empire.

New victories were urgently needed; and, lacking time to train the new recruits properly, the emperor would be forced to open a German campaign in 1813 with an army consisting mainly of young, inexperienced conscripts – and practically without trained cavalry. This need would be felt at Leipzig, where Napoleon kept most of his cavalry in reserve (a decision that probably saved his army at Hanau two weeks later).

Another problem Napoleon had to face was that he had also lost in Russia the faithful nucleus of his army, the cadres around whom he had previously been able to rebuild the Grande Armée. Most of the surviving NCOs were now promoted to the officer ranks, or were needed with the army in the field; and this would have damaging consequences for the process of training the new recruits at the depots.

THE DECREE

On 3 April 1813, following Napoleon's decision, the Senatus Consulte ordered the creation of four regiments of Gardes d'honneur, and two days later the decree was proclaimed. Twenty-four articles were needed to describe the organisation of the new corps, and where the men were to be found.

The four regiments of Guards of Honour were to be formed from volunteers, born Frenchmen – i.e., born in the empire – and were to be clad in elegant hussar-style uniforms (*noblesse oblige* …). Their garrisons were to be at Versailles (1st Regiment), Metz (2nd), Tours (3rd), and Lyon (4th). Each regiment was to be composed of a staff of 65 men and 156 horses, and no less than ten squadrons. Each squadron was to consist of two companies, each of 122 men and 127 horses. The establishment of the 20 companies in each regiment would be 2,440 men with 2,540 horses, the staff bringing the total to 2,505 men with 2,696 horses. His four regiments of Guards of Honour would together bring the emperor 10,000 well-equipped and mounted men, who would in due course provide the leadership cadres for his armies. The regimental colonels were chosen from among divisional or brigadier generals; the majors were colonels in the Line, though all the other officers would keep the same rank as they held in the Line.

Aged between 19 and 30 years old, the 'fine flower' of the empire who were summoned to join the new corps were to be unmarried and without a profession (the age limits were later relaxed to between 17 and 35 years). Who could volunteer to become a Guard of Honour? The élite and their sons, meaning members of the Legion of Honour or of the Imperial Order of the Reunion; Knights, Barons, Counts and even Dukes of the Empire; members of the departmental or district electoral councils, and councillors of the 'good' cities of the empire. In practice even administrators were acceptable to volunteer, and the definition of 'sons' stretched to include nephews.

Unsurprisingly, soldiers who were serving or had served in the French armies were also welcome, as were their sons; and so were current or former officers in one of the foreign allied armies. For these valuable veterans the age limit was raised as high as 45 years. And then there were the citizens, or the sons of the citizens, who paid the highest income taxes in their department or city – if they had the means, even these classes were allowed to enter the Guards of Honour.

One of the articles stated that the enlisted men had to pay for their uniform, horse and equipment themselves. The chancelleries of the Orders would provide financial support to their members who did not have the means to pay for their equipment. It was stated that the Guards of Honour would receive the same pay as the Chasseurs à cheval of the Imperial Guard; and that after 12 months' service in the ranks they would automatically be promoted to *sous-lieutenant*.

Drawing of a Guard of Honour by A.van Hammée. This trooper is shown in the standard full dress uniform that was more or less the same for all four regiments. However, coming from all corners of the empire, the men displayed many differences in exact shades and cloth qualities. Note the slung carbine, the *pique*-shaped braid motif on the thighs, and the tasselled hussar-style boots. (Collection of Belgian Royal Army Museum, Brussels)

General J.L.Lepic (1765–1827). This veteran of all the major campaigns of the Revolution and Empire became in 1805 the colonel-major of the Grenadiers à cheval of the Imperial Guard, and later a brigade general. Promoted divisional general in February 1813, and colonel of the 2e Gardes d'honneur, he suffered greatly from his wounds, in particular a severe head wound received in Russia which prevented him from wearing a hat. A combination of agonising headaches, gout, and increasing mental instability reduced his ability to command the regiment, and he was transferred to an administrative command with the 21st Military District at Bourges – a sad end to a long and glorious career. (Collection of Belgian Royal Army Museum, Brussels)

Each regiment was to enlist soldiers from different parts of the empire, and every department received instructions about the contingents of guardsmen that they had to muster:

The 1st Regiment was to be organised with volunteers from the 1st Military Division (Paris), the 14th (Caen), the 15th (Rouen), the 16th (Lille), the 24th (Brussels), and the 30th (Rome). The quotas for these areas totalled between 1,248 and 2,496 men.

The 2nd Regiment would receive volunteers from the 2nd Military Division (Mézières), the 3rd (Metz), the 4th (Nancy) the 5th (Strasbourg), the 17th (Amsterdam), the 18th (Dijon), the 25th (Wesel), the 26th (Mainz), and the 28th (Genoa), totalling between 1,205 and 2,410 men.

The 3rd Regiment would draw upon the 10th Military Division (Toulouse), the 11th (Bordeaux), the 12th (La Rochelle), the 13th (Rennes), the 20th (Périgueux), the 22nd (Tours), the 29th (Florence), and the 31st (Groningen), totalling between 1,305 and 2,610 men.

The 4th Regiment would take volunteers from the 6th Military Division (Besançon), the 7th (Grenoble), the 8th (Toulon), the 9th (Montpellier), the 19th (Lyon), the 21st (Bourges), the 23rd (Bastia), the 27th (Turin), and the 32nd (Hamburg), totalling between 1,242 and 2,484 men.

On 7 April 1813 the presses of the imperial printing office in Paris began turning out the decree; it would not only give the imperial administrators a lot of work, but would also cause the departmental prefects many headaches. From the River Elbe to the Pyrenees and from the coast of Friesland to the Tiber, it would agitate the ruling classes of the empire. For years such men had succeeded in buying 'proxies' to serve in the imperial armies in place of their sons – though sometimes at heavy cost. But now they had to obey: their own flesh and blood was summoned to the ranks, and this sacrifice turned many of them against the regime. In practice this ostensibly volunteer corps could not really be created out of spontaneous patriotic élan, and very soon the prefects were forced to 'appoint' volunteers, who therefore felt themselves more hostages than real soldiers.

Leadership

Commanding officers with famous historical family names were selected to lead the regiments, in order to attract even members of the old nobility. General of Division Count Defrance was appointed to the command of the Division of Guards of Honour. The 60-year-old Gen. Count de Pully was chosen to command the 1st Regiment; Gen. Baron Lepic, the 2nd; Gen. Count de Ségur – the son of Napoleon's Grand Master of Ceremonies – the 3rd; and Gen. Count Saint-Sulpice, the 4th Regiment.

Suitable cadres were in short supply, however; and each time the emperor asked for squadrons to be sent to join the field army, the colonels replied that they needed hand-picked soldiers, experienced NCOs and officers from the Line to train and lead the new recruits. This would remain a problem throughout the whole history of the regiments of Guards of Honour.

On 14 May 1813, in order to meet the urgent need for officers, Napoleon authorised the colonels to commission officers for their regiments. Squadron commanders (*chefs d'escadron* – i.e. majors) had to be French born, current or former members of the army, with an income of between 5,000 and 6,000 francs, and devoted to the emperor. Captains, lieutenants and sub-lieutenants were to be chosen by the regimental administration council, which consisted of the colonel, the two majors and the squadron commanders. Initially they were to look within the regiment for Guards of Honour who were eligible for promotion and had already held rank in the French or a foreign allied army.

By this date, throughout the empire, young men – volunteers or appointed – were being organised into detachments ready to march off to one of the four regimental depots.

RECRUITMENT

It was not an easy task for the departmental prefects to find the required numbers of men, but for the moment there was little reason for complaint. Just one month after the decree a total of 446 men had volunteered; four days later 1,166 names had been recorded, of whom 831 were volunteers; and within a week these numbers had tripled. By late May 1813 no less than 40 departments had already reached the maximum numbers required. Only one department – the Bouches de l'Elbe, with Hamburg as capital – was having real problems finding volunteers or suitable men; but by then, Russian troops were already occupying part of the department.

On 24 October 1813 the Ministry of the Interior could proudly announce to the emperor that the 1st Regiment (Versailles) had – on paper – 2,393 men; the 2nd (Metz), 2,417 men; the 3rd (Tours), 2,695 men; and the 4th (Lyon), 2,555 men, making a total of 10,060 men. In all, 6,837 men were delivered by the French departments; 1,232 by the Italian departments, Corsica and the Roman departments or former Papal States; 1,165 by the Belgian departments; 524 by the Dutch departments; and 302 by the German departments. These promised numbers were somewhat deceptive, however: they were the totals reported by the prefects for the numbers of men who left the departments for the depots. In reality some of them never arrived or, once they had reported to the garrison, were found unfit for military service. By 24 November, 9,714 men had been sent to the regimental depots, but only 9,129 would actually serve in the Guards of Honour.

Portrait of G.V.Lecoq de Biéville, a guardsman in the 1er Régiment des Gardes d'honneur. Born at Caen, Normandy, in 1783, he entered the Guards of Honour on 13 July 1813, and is recorded as being 1.7m tall. He passed into the 1st Scouts Regiment of the Imperial Guard in December 1813; in May 1814 he returned home without permission – as did so many soldiers after Napoleon's first abdication. He returned to the army for the Hundred Days campaign of 1815, serving with the Grenadiers à cheval of the Imperial Guard. Since most of the Guards of Honour were financially better off than the majority of soldiers, many could afford uniforms of fashionable, even dandified cut. Lecoq de Biéville displays a stylish high collar, a shako worn at a jaunty angle, and a pelisse slung over the left shoulder. Note the regimental number '1' cut out of the shield under the Imperial Eagle on his shako plate, with the red cloth body showing through. (Collection of Belgian Royal Army Museum, Brussels)

It was naturally easier to find volunteers within the French borders of 1792 than in the annexed departments; in France proper, only the traditionally royalist departments such as Brittany and the Vendée failed to respond well. Even so, Brittany's five departments were still able to send some 540 men to the 3rd Regiment's depot at Tours – though in due course some of them revealed themselves to have a different agenda than serving the emperor. It was easier in the departments of the Ile-de-France around Paris: these levied 524 guardsmen, of which 160 came from the Seine department alone.

Throughout the empire, men volunteered or were chosen, and once dressed, mounted and equipped they were sent to their respective depots. In the Nord department the first 15 volunteers, among them two sons of the mayor of Dunkirk, left for the 1st Regiment at Versailles on 1 May. One month later, the minimum required for the department was reached – 100 men, and all volunteers; 60 were already marching towards Versailles, and the other 40 would leave shortly. In Normandy things did not proceed so smoothly; it was with some difficulty that the five Norman departments gathered the required 600 men for the 1st Regiment.

Italy

Outside France, in Italy, the prefects found the men needed in spite of the hesitation of some local councils and leading families. For the 27th, 28th and 29th Military Divisions special measures were decreed. Large numbers of men were already serving in one of the local Italian Guard units (e.g. Guard of Honour of Turin), in the Vélites, and as lieutenants and sub-lieutenants of the 14th Hussars. Stationed in Mainz, these men could apply to serve in the Guards of Honour and their numbers would be deducted from the required local quotas. Forty-four of them took the opportunity to transfer into the 4th Regiment. In the meantime the first detachments left Italy for France: 50 men from Piedmont left Turin on 23 June; and on 15 July another 81, commanded by a captain and former officer in the Gendarmerie, left Alessandria. The Stura department sent four different detachments to Lyon between 17 June and 24 July. Those who travelled from Tuscany and Rome took their time, only reaching Tours in October. In total the Italian departments mustered 204 men from Rome and Trasimène (the former Papal States) for the 1st Regiment; 236 men from Genoa and 144 from Piedmont went to the 2nd; 256 men from Tuscany were selected for the 3rd; and 356 men mainly from Piedmont were directed to the 4th Regiment.

Switzerland

In Switzerland, the department of Leman immediately found 40 volunteers against a maximum of 47 men required. In Geneva, capital

Mounted trooper of the 1st Regiment. The Dutch guards-man A.van den Broecke was one of the first appointees – rather than volunteers – to reach the regimental depot at Versailles. A second physical examination there revealed him to be unfit for active service, and he ended up in the depot company. Without much to do, he travelled widely around Paris, Antwerp and Brussels. Later he would be taken into custody when Dutch origin became sufficient reason for the French to doubt a man's loyalty. Van den Broecke kept a journal that he illustrated with six watercolours showing his friends in uniform and scenes of military life. This one shows the full dress uniform; note the red-tipped green shako plume with its red pompon, the white sheepskin shabraque, and the cylindrical portmanteau with the regimental number. (Collection of Zeeuwse Bibliotheek, Holland)

of the department, after a parade in full dress, the prefect gathered the new recruits in the dining room of the prefecture and before the meal he offered a toast to the emperor's health: 'Guards of Honour, élite of the department of Leman, go and join the rest of the Empire – go and show that you are willing to compete for the love of the great man who presides over our destiny!'

Among these recruits we find the name of one Frederic-August Cramer (or Kramer), chosen for the 4th Regiment. Some days after receiving the decree the prefect of the department, Baron Capelle, had come to see Cramer's father. He reassured the young man's parents that the Guards of Honour, whose future task would be to act as Life Guards for the King of Rome (the son of the emperor), would be kept away from the hazards of battle. Having five children and being a member of the imperial administration, Cramer *père* fell into the category of men mentioned in the decree. Frederic-August, aged just 17 and flattered by the imperial summons, agreed without hesitation.

His uniforms were made according to the models sent from Lyon, and for the first time in his life he found himself responsible for the daily care of a horse. At daybreak on 2 June 1813 the young Cramer left the military stables with the rest of his detachment. The band of the National Guard joined them, their music drowning out more than one murmur of anxiety. Six days later they arrived at Lyon, where they would be quartered in the Caserne de la Charité near Bellecourt. Cramer, thanks to the influence of the prefect, would be promoted quarter-master; his 26-year-old friend de Sonnaz – whose father was a former governor and general in service of the King of Sardinia – became a sergeant-major.

The two friends from Geneva would serve in the 2nd Squadron, com-manded by the Count de Saluces, from Piedmont; Cramer's company was commanded by Capt. de Montillet du Champ d'Or, who had served in the army of the Condé against the Revolution, but who had now joined the Guards of Honour in order to escape from his domestic problems. The first lieutenant was a certain Colin, described as a rough hoodlum. The second lieutenant was a good man named Riedmatten, a former lieutenant in the Valaison Battalion. The two sergeants were Parisian dandies, both in their early thirties (one of them, with the oddly British-sounding name of Onslow, would later become a famous musician). Among the rest of the cadres of the company we find men such as Cuneo d'Ornano, a small man of the same age as Cramer, who came from Corsica and was a distant relative of the Bonapartes; De Fenouil de Marbœuf; Sauvaigne, from Nice; and Brion, from Artois, who would be killed at Dresden. The 4th, like all the other regiments, presented a mixture of nationalities, cultures, classes and languages.

Another Swiss department, Simplon, only had to send 12 men and found them without problems; all were equipped, mounted and dressed in Lyon at the expense of the department.

The Low Countries

The nine Belgian departments mostly found the required men without excessive difficulties. The Dyle department found 20 volunteers and had to appoint 56 other men to make up the decreed quota. The Deux-Nèthes department took four months to find 88 men; they left in five

Corporal of the 4th Regiment in summer campaign dress, wearing the dolman with overalls reinforced with black leather. Full equipment is carried, with the exception of the saddle pistols. Over the pouch belt is buttoned the broad sling belt to which the carbine was hooked. NCOs wore the same uniform as the troopers with the difference that all braiding, lace and shako cords were in silver or, according to some sources, mixed silver and green. Rank distinctions were as for hussars: corporals wore a silver chevron above the cuffs and a silver band at the top of the shako. (Collection of Belgian Royal Army Museum, Brussels)

parties, arriving at Versailles between 19 May and 5 September. The Escaut department found their required 152 men.

In Holland, the prefects had to muster 398 guardsmen of whom 14 were chosen for the 1st Regiment, 316 for the 2nd, and 68 for the 3rd Regiment. As a proportion of the populations these were not high numbers, but the administration nevertheless had serious problems in finding them. On 2 June, the 12 men who left Middelburg consisted largely of inn and restaurant keepers – hardly the class envisaged; once at Versailles, ten of them were rejected and packed off to join Line regiments because they lacked the necessary standard of education. At Arnhem, in the department of the Yssel Supérieur, only three volunteers offered their services out of a total of 44 men required. However, in the Bouches de l'Yssel department the prefect was able to find the decreed maximum of 31 guardsmen destined for the 3rd Regiment.

In Friesland, in the far north of Holland, the first of three detachments was also ready to march towards Tours. Their departure was delayed because they had to wait for the arrival of their uniforms from The Hague, and for the shakos, sent on 29 June from Paris. At last the first 15 guardsmen, commanded by one Van Hylckama and including the single genuine volunteer from the department – S.H.Manger – left Leeuwarden on 12 July. A second party of 15 men would leave on the 20th, and a third, of just five guardsmen, on 29 July. One G.Buma, the son of the mayor of Leeuwarden, tried to escape military service on the grounds of health problems; invited to come to the prefecture, he found his equipment, uniform and horse waiting for him there. After a parade in full dress he was sent off to Tours with the rest of his party, arriving on 20 August. Once at the depot Buma was assigned to the 6th Squadron of the 3rd Regiment; with this unit he left for Mainz in mid-September, arriving there on 20 October 1813.

In Groningen, in the department of Ems Occidental, the minimum quota was 22 men. These were found, and on 30 June a first departmental detachment of 35 men left Groningen for Tours. By 20 July a total of 54 guardsmen had left the department, 11 men more than the maximum required. One of them was the 22-year-old Albertus Dassen.

Like most educated men, Albertus took the opportunity of the five-week journey to Tours to visit places of interest along the way. In Antwerp they visited the churches, the town hall and the naval base; in Brussels they visited the imperial palace of Laeken, where they were able to see the bedrooms of the emperor and empress. Everywhere they were billeted in lodgings normally reserved for officers; their only complaint

was that life was expensive. In Paris – the storehouse of Europe's treasures – they visited the Palais Royal, famous cafés like 'La Belle Limonadière', the Jardin des Plantes, the Invalides, the Musée Impérial and the Panthéon. On 30 July they left for Saint-Cloud and Versailles, and on 6 August they arrived in Tours. Here military life became a reality for the tourists. The day after their arrival Gen. Count de Ségur, colonel of the 3rd Regiment, inspected them. The guardsmen from Groningen were kept together in the same squadron. The whole day was taken up with drill, and they only came off duty between 9 and 10pm. At the end of August, Gen. de Ségur was able to report that they were ready to join the army. The guardsmen, however, did not share his opinion.

On 15 July, 121 guardsmen had left Amsterdam for Metz. Even when the maximum requirement had been reached, the prefect De Celles, a strong supporter of Napoleon's regime, appointed another 35 men – a decision which did nothing for his popularity among the inhabitants of the city.

Germany

In war-torn Germany, Hamburg had been evacuated by the French and was unable to organise a detachment for the Guards of Honour. At Bremen, in the department of Bouches du Weser, 78 guardsmen were found and sent off for Lyon. In Lippe no volunteers were found, and 54 men were chosen for the 2nd Regiment. At Osnabruck, in the department of Ems Supérieur, a detachment of 30 guardsmen left for Lyon on 25 August. In the Rhin et Moselle department (Koblenz) the authorities also found the required numbers of men. At Mainz, Mont-Tonnerre, only 64 men could be found out of the required maximum of 203 guardsmen.

At Trier in the Saar department 39 men were ready to leave on 18 June; a second detachment with 23 men would soon follow. One of the first volunteers was Jean-Jacques-Toussaint Lamby, aged 18, who presented himself to the prefect, Baron de Sainte-Suzanne, declaring his zeal 'to come to the aid of those brave men who were already serving'. From the moment when they received horses they had to parade every day before a certain Desguiots, a former hussar, and in a short time they would be initiated into the military life. Desguiots, temporarily promoted sergeant, became commander of the detachment; Jean Lamby would act as corporal until they reached Metz. But before leaving Trier the men of the detachment were given an impressive send-off.

They entertained many members of the city administration and local society at a farewell ball on the evening of 14 June. Two days later Baron Mannai, Bishop of Trier and Councillor of State, hosted a banquet for them; after the meal toasts were proposed, and there were repeated shouts of *'Vive l'Empereur!'* The bishop urged the soldiers to stay always loyal to 'the Emperor and Honour', the sole basis for all French military action. On the day of departure the prefect offered the guardsmen breakfast, and again they shouted

'Vive l'Empereur!' They were then assembled in front of the prefecture, and the prefect – with a heavily embroidered flag in his hand – reminded them once again of their duty to Country and Emperor, to which they responded by waving their swords in the air and shouting 'Vive l'Empereur, vive notre préfet!' At last the order to march was given. Joined by the prefect and the city's military commanders, who accompanied the column as far as the border of the department, the first detachment left Trier – apparently with heavy hearts, despite their champagne breakfast.

Following the road via Grevenmachen, they met up in Luxemburg with the first detachment from the Roër department. Once arrived in Metz, garrison of the 2nd Regiment, they were inspected by Col. Lepic. His welcome was not quite what the guardsmen had expected – their commanding officer openly cursed the prefect of the Saar for having failed to obey the uniform and equipment regulations.

*   *   *

It was hardly surprising that in some parts of the empire the enthusiasm for service was not as great as had been expected, forcing some prefects to exercise inventiveness. In some cases proxies were found to serve as replacements at high cost, even though this was against the law. For this reason there could be found in the ranks of the regiments the sons of peasants, labourers, even sailors – much to the disgust of the more refined volunteers. In the 4th Regiment some complained that they were surrounded by uneducated men. General de Pully complained in a letter to his colleague of the 3rd Regiment that he had had to reject individuals who were not suitable for the corps. Some prefects also failed in their duty in sending the men without proper equipment, and this unbalanced the financial situation of the regiments. In short, a lot of time was wasted discussing and finding remedies for problems whose solutions had been decreed in advance but not obeyed by the departmental authorities. In some cases horses even arrived without Guards of Honour!

At their depots, where the soldiers exercised every day, the quality of some uniforms showed that the owners in fact came from the lowest social classes. Theft was rife among the guardsmen, and having money was – as always – important: it could buy the services of the poorer guardsmen to take over the menial duties for richer men. As most of the wealthier guardsmen were accustomed to having servants at home, they had even asked the departmental prefects whether they could take them with them. Some simply told their servants to follow the detachment to the depot, and once there – since there were no official quarters for them – some guardsmen rented private rooms where they kept a servant.

In late 1810 new regulations were issued regarding shakos. All cords and tassels were (officially) abolished, to curb extravagant excesses in uniform style. The shako itself became more elegant in shape, moving towards the later *shako rouleau*. This white metal plate shows the legend 'GARDE D'HONNEUR' in the curl of the bugle-horn. The metal chin scales are a mixture of white metal and brass. The cockade is a painted metal rosette. (Collection of Belgian Royal Army Museum, Brussels)

Stable duties were not to the taste of the more privileged young men; and in July 1813 Napoleon conceded, at the request of the Guards of honour, that servants should be allowed in the regiments. A regulation stipulated that a groom (nicknamed a 'Tartar') should be responsible for the horses of each two guardsmen. Mounted himself, the groom was to be armed with a hussar sabre and a pistol. His headdress was to be a black shako; the chasseur-style light cavalry jacket and Hungarian breeches were to be in grey cloth, with collar, facings, piping and breeches stripes in green; a white waistcoat and black hussar boots, black leather equipment, and a grey cloak with white buttons completed his outfit.

UNIFORMS

According to the decree and organisation of the Corps of Guards of Honour, the Ministry of the Interior wrote to the prefects specifying that:

'The buttons are in silver or silver-plated, like those of the officers. The braid and lace are in white wool for the uniforms and in white cord for the shako. The shako will be as the model you will receive; but the shako plate, the chin chains and the other metal pieces on it will be silver-plated.

'The shako will have a green plume with the tip in a different colour for each regiment. This will be red for the 1st, imperial blue for the 2nd, yellow for the 3rd, and white for the 4th regiment. The plume will have a pompon as base. This will be in a different colour for each company. The metal ornaments on the sabretache will be silver-plated.'

The intention was that every Guard of Honour had to pay for his own uniform, equipment and horse, and was to leave his department fully equipped and in uniform. In practice, every time a new detachment arrived at the depots the officers had reason to complain. Sometimes the men had no shakos and arrived wearing civilian hats; some wore the wrong boots; and others wore mixtures of military and civilian clothing. The 4th Regiment was the worst of all, according to a report by Gen. Nansouty; some Italians in this regiment had not a single piece of uniform or equipment with them, while 86 of them asked to be sent back home so

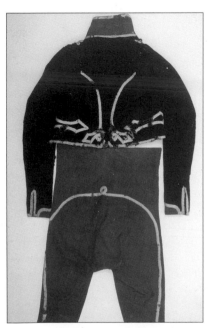

Front and rear views of the dolman and breeches of F.X.Goethals, a Belgian volunteer in the Guards of Honour who had a horse killed under him at Leipzig. The style of hussar uniforms changed during the last years of the Empire: dolmans became shorter and trousers more high-waisted. The dark green dolman has red collar and shallow cuff facings, white braid edgings, five rows of white metal half-ball buttons, and white cord frogging – just visible are the upper ends carried up to finish in trefoil knots high on the narrow shoulders. The red breeches are of the tight-fitting Hungarian pattern, with white braid on the outer seams uniting at the back in a circle; this normally curled downwards below the braid, but is occasionally seen placed above it as here. The vents of the front 'fall' flap of the breeches are surrounded with white braid *piques*, and the buttons are covered with red cloth. The white braid was replaced on officers' uniforms with silver lace, gold and silver for majors, or gold for commanding officers. (Collection of Belgian Royal Army Museum, Brussels)

that they could have their uniforms made – once fitted out, they would of course return to the regiment. One wonders!

Shakos were made too large and pads had to be ordered to make them fit; trousers were too short, and so on. With guardsmen coming from all corners of Europe the colours of the materials were of different shades and the quality varied; on parade, one saw many shades of red and green in a single regiment. Although officers and some rich troopers had finely cut uniforms in the best possible materials, conforming with their means and social status, many of the guardsmen were badly or incompletely dressed, and equipment was lacking. In general any procurement that had been left to the departmental authorities had been skimped, from carelessness, resentment or 'economy'. Once the first fully equipped squadrons were being sent to join the field army, things got worse. Most of the time the majority of the men in the ranks of the regiments presented a poor appearance.

The normal uniform regulations were as follows:

Headgear

More voluminous than the regulation model of other corps, the **shako** was of leather covered with red cloth and decorated with white piping. The band was of black leather; the front peak was edged in silver-plated metal; the cockade was of cloth.

The cord festoon was white. In the 3rd Regiment the two plaited cords were worn across the front, covering part of the plate. Racquets ('flounders') were worn on the left, the reverse of the practice in the Line. The cord was attached with a small pin on the inside of the shako; on some models a large pin was stitched to the white piping; and some had small hooked stars similar to those worn in the Line.

The dark green pelisse from the uniform on page 13, braided and corded like the dolman but without red facings. At the end of the Empire these too were shorter, and designed so that only the top buttons could be fastened. Instead of the normal black fur trim this example has dark brown, probably at the personal choice of Guardsman Goethals. The fur has been torn off the collar at some point, exposing the white lining. (Collection of Belgian Royal Army Museum, Brussels)

The vulture feather plumes were about 56cm (22ins) high, dark green, with the distinctive regimental colour at the top – one-fifth of the total height: red, light blue, yellow and white for the 1st–4th Regiments respectively. The plume was attached by a bone stem into a sheath inside or outside the shako. Company pompons were pierced to receive the full dress plume, but the former had no stem and could not be worn alone.

A self-coloured 'ball-and-tuft' pompon in the regimental colour was worn with service dress. On campaign the shako was covered with black waxed cloth.

The **stable cap** was of dragoon style, with a turban and wing in dark green piped in scarlet; white piping was stitched to the top edge of the turban, and the lining was canvas.

Dolman

The dolman was in dark green, lined with canvas. The collar and the facings were scarlet. The front bore 18 rows of white cord. The false pockets and collar and cuff edging were in white braid. The buttons, like those of the officers, were plain, in

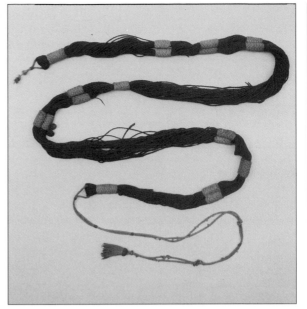

Dolmans were reinforced inside with leather patches; Goethals' has a deep strip of pale red leather around the waist. Note also the way that the front flap of the breeches covered the central fly opening. (Collection of Belgian Royal Army Museum, Brussels)

ABOVE RIGHT This crimson and white barrel-sash wrapped three times around the waist, with a total length of 2.60m (8.5ft). (Collection of Belgian Royal Army Museum, Brussels)

silver-plated metal. The dolman had 91 buttons in all, of which 72 were of medium size for the two rows on either side of the breast, 18 were large for the middle row, and one medium for the left shoulder strap.

Pelisse

The pelisse was in dark green, lined with white flannel, and edged on the collar, the front edges and sleeve cuffs with black fur. Like the dolman it had 18 lines of white cording, but with five rows each of 18 buttons.

Waistcoat

The vest was scarlet and sleeveless. The edge of the collar, the waist and the false pockets were piped in white. The breast bore 18 rows of white cord with five rows of medium size buttons.

Legwear

The **breeches** were of 'Hungarian' style, scarlet with white braids along the outer seams, and decorated with white pointed *piques* motifs on the front of the thighs.

A hussar-style **barrel sash** was worn, made of 44 crimson cords with 20 white 'barrels'; 2.60 metres long, the sash was worn wrapped three times around the body over the waistcoat.

Light cavalry **boots** in black leather were specified. Some had white braid trim with tassels at the top edge; others had simple black leather tassels stitched to the front; some boots were also worn without any ornament. The heel was reinforced with a 'horseshoe' and a fixed spur.

Fatigue and field clothing

The **stable jacket** – including the collar, facings and shoulder straps – was made in the same dark green cloth as the rest of the uniform.

It fastened with 15 medium size buttons and was worn over canvas stable trousers. The voluminous cavalry **greatcoat** or sleeved cloak was made from green cloth, with a straight collar fastened with two small tabs. For field dress the red breeches were replaced by green **riding overalls**, fastening up the outside by means of 18 large buttons stitched into a stripe of scarlet cloth. They had a 25mm-wide leather instep strap, and buckskin reinforcement sewn into the crotch and inner legs. Towards the end of the Empire the trousers were made of grey cloth.

Equipment

The hussar model **cartridge pouch** was worn, a wooden box covered in black leather; the flap was fastened with a buckle stitched under the box. The **pouch belt** was in white hide. The **carbine sling** was in white hide with a square buckle. The **sword belt** was of hussar type in white hide, adjustable by means of a buckle on the right side. Attached to rings on the left side, three slings supported the sabretache and two others the sabre scabbard. The belt also had a bayonet frog with leather sheath.

The **sabretache** was in varnished black leather, without embroidery or piping. It bore a crowned eagle in silver-plated copper, surmounting the regimental number. Three brass rings received the slings to the sword belt.

Armament

At first this comprised a light cavalry sabre with white sword knot; an An IX cavalry musket with bayonet; and a pair of An XIII pistols. This full equipment was rarely seen, however.

Horse equipment

The portmanteau was in green cloth with white braid stitched in a circle to the ends, surrounding the regimental number cut from white cloth. The shabraque was in white sheepskin, of hussar style. The saddlery and harness were also of hussar type, in black leather.

Trumpeters

All regiments wore the 'Imperial livery' like the light horse regiments of the Line. The dark green dolman and pelisse bore seven chevrons on each arm in the Imperial braid. This was yellow with scarlet edges, divided into rectangles by transverse black lines, alternate rectangles bearing a green eagle and a green cypher 'N'. A variation showed narrower scarlet edges and the 'N' in yellow on a green ground; the eagle remained green on yellow.

Later the four regiments would adopt distinctive uniforms in the style of the Imperial Guard trumpeters, who wore light blue. The dolman became light blue, perhaps worn in combination with a scarlet pelisse; a white busby with a red bag might also replace the shako.

Officers

Similar uniform to troopers but of finer cloth, with silver piping and braid replacing white, and with individual variations in detail. Colonels wore white plumes, and two silver bands round the upper

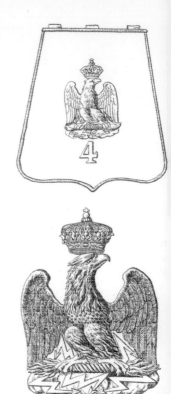

Sabretache in black leather, with silver-plated crowned eagle and regimental number; and detail of Imperial eagle badge.

Officer's black leather sabretache with silver lace border and silver-plated eagle, shield and crown badge.

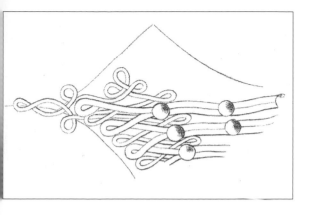

NCO's dolman cording, upper outside corner showing trefoil termination.

Silvered shako plate from the 2nd Regiment of Guards of Honour.

edge of the shako; the pompon at the base of officers' plumes was also silver. Some officers wore a fur colpack (busby) with a scarlet bag piped and tasselled silver. All leather equipment was red with silver braiding and ornaments. Hussar-style boots were worn in black or red leather with silver trim and tassels; some officers even wore light green boots, with gloves in the same colour. Horse harness was as luxurious as for hussar officers. Shabraques were in dark green cloth piped in red and braided silver; senior officers sometimes displayed gold braid.

The prices of some privately ordered troopers' uniform items of fine quality were as follows:

Dolman, with silk & silver details	175 francs
Red waistcoat	30 francs
Waistcoat with braiding	75 francs
Red breeches, with silk & silver details	75 francs
Overcoat	120 francs
Forage cap	30 francs
Green riding overalls	75 francs
Shako with plume	61 francs
2 pairs of boots, spurs, gloves	66 francs
Sabre	25 francs
Also: grey breeches for groom	48 francs
Grey coat for groom	48 francs

Later a service uniform was introduced consisting of a green dress coat with scarlet collar facings and lapel piping and white shoulder knots. This was worn with green breeches with white braid motifs, and a scarlet waistcoat with white braids. The hat cockade was attached by a white wool loop held by a silver-plated button.

ORGANISING THE REGIMENTS

Given the army's serious lack of cavalry, the intention was that from the moment the Guards of Honour were fully equipped and knew more or less how to stay in the saddle, they would be sent to join the field army in Germany, the rest of their training being carried out during their march. It was on 19 June 1813, only two months after the decree, that the first detachment of the 1st Squadron of the 1st Regiment, led by the squadron commander Etienne de Pully (son of the regimental colonel, Gen. de Pully) left Versailles for Mainz, followed by the rest of the squadron some four days later. It was Napoleon's intention to have the four first squadrons of each ten-squadron regiment assembled at Mainz as soon as possible. Later, as and when other squadrons were brought to a state of readiness at the depots, they could join their regiments there.

By 31 July 1813 the four first squadrons of the 1st Regiment were at Mainz or on their way. Colonel-Major de Castellane (a future marshal under Napoleon III) was surprised by the lack of military knowledge displayed by officers and men alike, and astonished that they had been sent forward to the army in this state: the men of the 4th Squadron were not even capable of leading a horse. The 25-year-old officer complained mainly about the short time he was given to teach his soldiers horsemanship; in his opinion even men who had been forced into the army could become good soldiers, as long as a realistic period of time was devoted to training them.

From Tours the 1st Squadron of the 3rd Regiment, led by Maj. Darbaud-Misson, left for Mainz, where they awaited the arrival of the 2nd Squadron before proceeding together to Gotha, where they were expected on 8 September 1813. The first squadron of the 4th Regiment soon followed from Lyon, after taking two days to prepare for departure. At 6am on a fine morning the troopers were lined up on the barrack square of the Caserne de la Charité, watched from every vantage point by a crowd of citizens. The general did not make a speech, but when he gave the command to march the trumpets sounded and everyone, soldiers and citizens together, cried *'Vive l'Empereur!'* Young Frederic-August Cramer of the 2nd Squadron was glad that he was not with the first detachment to leave, so he could see this imposing spectacle several times over. On 6 July it would be his turn to get on the road for Germany; his party travelled via Besançon and Strasbourg, arriving at Mainz on 4 August.

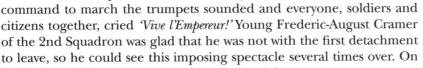

One by one, the regiments sent their squadrons to Mainz and from there to join the army. They marched as Provisional Regiments, resuming their proper titles when they reached Gotha. Arriving at Mainz, where he hoped for some rest, Cramer wrote to his family: 'We have just received our orders. We are being sent to Gotha in all haste and without a single day of rest – we have just two hours before leaving. The roads are packed with cavalry; the quartermasters are marching – as always – 24 hours in advance [of their units] but several together. I have seen a squadron of the Metz regiment [2nd], together with a regiment of Line cavalry, crossing the Rhine. It is a good moment when one sets foot across the border of France. The Emperor said that he will have an army of 400,000 men on his birthday.'

On 2 August Col.Maj. de Castellane was already organising the 14th Company at Versailles, a difficult task given that the 1st Regiment still suffered from a chronic lack of experienced officers and NCOs. He could not understand why they were refused decent cadres seconded from the Line. With an armature of such soldiers, he felt confident that he could make fine regiments

of the human material at his disposal, since most of the Guards of Honour were better educated and learned faster than other soldiers; but they had far too few instructors, and not enough time for instruction.

Meanwhile Gen. de Ségur, colonel of the 3rd Regiment, was complaining about the prefect of the Loire-et-Cher department; he wrote that the men he received from there were ridiculously small in stature, and so young that they would have to be kept at the depot rather than being sent on active service. Many of them were not suited for military life, and ended up in hospital after a period of training. As a consequence the other men at the depot each had to take care of two horses, which took up even more of the already inadequate time available for training them.

On 12 August 1813 one of the few Dutch volunteers, the 15-year-old Jacobus Salverda of the 4th Regiment, wrote to his parents that his unit were quartered in the ruins of the Marmouillet monastery. They slept four to a room, on straw mattresses covered by old blankets with holes he could stick two fingers through, some of them patched with old socks instead of blanket cloth. At 5am they had to get up and groom and feed the horses; then they were drilled. At 10am they had breakfast – a piece of boiled meat and half a bottle of wine; dinner was at 4pm, consisting of soup and meat. This all sounds perfectly normal for a Napoleonic soldier, but apparently came as something of a shock to young Salverda; he complained that he was leading a dog's life – but could still find pleasure in it.

At the barracks of the 1st Regiment in Versailles, new detachments arrived from Rome, Amsterdam, Piedmont and the centre of France. Within 24 hours of their arrival at the depot they were organised into companies and squadrons, and from the moment that they could mount a horse and knew the basics they were sent to Mainz. A detachment of some hundred horses was sometimes commanded by an officer who had never before served in the cavalry, and the NCOs were appointed from among the recruits more or less by pointing at likely looking men and saying, 'You, you're the sergeant-major; you're a sergeant, and you're a corporal'.

Occasionally things went better than this, however. On 27 August 1813 the 5th Squadron of the 1st Regiment left Versailles, commanded by Capt. de Beauregard. They were better disciplined and trained that most of the squadrons, thanks to the hard work of Adjutant-Major Sémin, who had come from the 13e Chasseurs à cheval – proof that good, experienced NCOs could do wonders.

On 30 August, the 5th Squadron of the 3rd Regiment, commanded by Sub-Lt. de France, left Tours for the army; in their ranks was the Dutchman Albertus Dassen from Groningen. On 15 September they reached Joinville, and Metz on the 21st.

General Dejean, field commander of the Guards of Honour Division, left Leipzig on 20 August with the first six squadrons, arriving at Dresden three days later. With him he had Col.Maj. de Pange of the 2nd Regiment, Col.Maj. de Saluces of the 3rd and Col.Maj. de Monteil of the 4th. Each of the six squadrons was led by its squadron commander except the 2nd of the 2nd Regiment, whose commander had been replaced and now served as a supernumerary. But with all these senior officers, Gen. Dejean still lacked lower-ranking officers and NCOs.

Little by little, the Guards of Honour were gathered around the emperor; but meanwhile, a confrontation was brewing back in France.

19

Conspiracy at Tours

Within the ranks of an under-officered corps with weak NCO cadres, drawn from the educated classes of a mixture of regional cultures – even nationalities – of which not all had much reason for loyalty to the empire, small signs of disaffection were only to be expected. They were duly noticed; but at Tours, where Gen. de Ségur's 3rd Regiment was quartered, things got out of hand.

Large parts of the regiment came from the Vendée region in the west of France, which had been a royalist heartland during the Revolution. The people of this area had taken up arms and resisted the Parisian government for several years; and this counter-revolution – which was finally crushed with great brutality – had been led by famous local families with names such as d'Elbée, de Charette, la Rochejaquelein and de Nétumières. As long as Napoleon held a winning hand and France was still powerful and victorious the province remained quiet – the Revolution had killed all the leaders of the Vendée. But now their sons and nephews were called to serve in the Guards of Honour. Royalist in heart and blood, they would only serve the emperor more or less grudgingly, and strictly in order to save France from defeat or invasion.

Guard of Honour at the charge, by Bastin. The red tip of his plume indicates the 1st Regiment. The white sheepskin shabraque, shown here with green edging, was in use by the rankers (but not the officers) of all four regiments. The flounders and tassels on his right shoulder may be a fantasy of the artist, as they were officially forbidden at this date, but such orders were sometimes disobeyed. (Collection of Belgian Royal Army Museum, Brussels)

While this potentially disaffected group were quartered in Tours, most of them in private apartments in the town and thus unsupervised during their free hours, an unknown man (said to have been a horse dealer) contacted some of them. During the last two weeks of August 1813, the guardsmen gathered daily at an inn called the Café Leblanc – the name of the proprietor – which was also known as the Café Militaire; it was in this building that the young de Nétumières had quarters. These gatherings usually involved about 20 Guards of Honour together with some civilians. The evenings fell into a pattern: the talented Guardsman de Barrau sang to entertain the company, wine was drunk, the young men laughed, talked – and made plans. As the weeks passed the talk became bolder.

Some spoke of taking prisoner their colonel and the local colonel of the Gendarmerie, seizing the regimental and town money chests, and marching back to the Vendée to organise an insurrection. This idea was abandoned as their ranks were thinned by the departure of some of the squadrons to join the army. Among the wilder suggestions were a plan to march with some 100 guardsmen to Saint-Cloud and capture the empress; and another, to ride to Valençay and liberate the deposed King of Spain from his imprisonment, escorting him and his family back to Spain. Some preferred a move towards Brittany: if they could reach Saint-Malo, perhaps they could contact England, and the émigré Gen. Moreau could lead some 30,000 French prisoners of war across the Channel to invade France? (They could not know that within a matter of days Moreau would be killed at Dresden while serving the Tsar.)

Wednesday 25 August 1813 was getting closer. In France, some people celebrated not their actual birthday but the name day of the saint after whom they were christened. Since 25 August was the day of St Louis, a famous medieval Crusader king of France, that was the day to celebrate everything these royalists stood for. Some 16 guardsmen gathered at the Café Militaire, among them Lt. de Lacarre, and the civilian younger brother of the influential de Charette. They had a large meal, and wine flowed generously; toasts were drunk to a squadron of the regiment whose good behaviour in the presence of the enemy had just been reported, and the newly promoted Sgt. Jamain's stripes were baptised with wine. As the drink went to their heads glasses were raised to Louis XVIII; there was excited talk about going over to the enemy the moment they crossed the Rhine on their way to join the army – even of assassinating Napoleon. It was agreed that they needed the support of influential members of the regiment including de Charette, de Marigny, de Boissimon and Delaunay.

The next morning's hangovers cooled the young men's mood considerably; but on 15 October the Café Militaire was closed down for a month by order of the police. Unknown to all from the colonel down, the Minister of Police had placed a man from the Vendée in the ranks of the 3rd Regiment as a spy. The minister informed Gen. de Ségur that his life was in danger, and Guards of Honour de Barrau, Majorel, de Boissimon, Domène and Frottier de Lacoste were arrested. Most of the arrests went unnoticed, but Frottier de Lacoste was taken away after an inspection, and his close friend de Nétumières saw him go. When he tried to intervene he was sent away by the colonel. Later de Nétumières' friends and family would claim that he was mentally unstable; he was certainly deeply upset, and made plans to liberate his friend.

General de Ségur, feeling insecure, had some gendarmes installed in and around his house. Nevertheless, when darkness fell a party of conspirators including de Nétumières, Bargain, la Barbelais and de Marigny armed themselves with pistols and somehow managed to enter their colonel's quarters without being noticed. Suddenly, Gen. de Ségur found himself confronted by de Nétumières; followed by Bargain, the ringleader aimed his pistol at de Ségur, with a sword hanging from the same wrist. He demanded that the colonel release de Lacoste; de Ségur refused, and ordered them to leave; and de Nétumières fired, slightly wounding the colonel. In the commotion, de Ségur drew his sword to defend himself; Bargain and de Nétumières tried twice more to shoot the colonel, but each time their pistols misfired. In moments the room filled with gendarmes, and de Nétumières and his accomplices were dragged away. All were imprisoned; and their lives were only saved by the fall of Napoleon in spring 1814.

It was only a few months later that this same regiment, commanded by its colonel General de Ségur, would fight so bravely at Rheims.

Officer of the Gardes d'honneur, 1814, in *tenue de route*, by L.Vallet. Officers wore more stylish uniforms, of better quality, more in vogue and more expensive. This officer wears the very popular *shako rouleau* of tall cylindrical shape, in the corps' distinctive scarlet with silver decorations. A crimson leather cover protects his expensive pouch belt; his green overalls have silver side-stripes. The officer's green shabraque has the lower corners hooked up to protect the silver embroidered crowned eagle emblems from wear and dirt – and perhaps also to hide this symbol of the Imperial Guard from the eyes of the enemy? (Collection of Belgian Royal Army Museum, Brussels)

THE 1813 CAMPAIGN

To Saxony

Five months had passed since Napoleon, crossing the Polish-Russian border, had given command of the remnants of the Grande Armée to his brother-in-law Murat. In that brief period he had restored order in the capital, regathered his energies, raised a new army, and marched back across the Rhine. Between 2 and 21 May 1813 he had inflicted a series of lightning defeats on the Russo-Prussian armies at Lützen, Bautzen and Würtschen.

On 8 May Napoleon had been at Dresden; on the 29th of that same month Marshal Ney's vanguard entered Breslau, while Davout recaptured Hamburg. The Allies agreed to an armistice, which was signed at Pleiswitz. Napoleon hoped that this respite would enable him to regroup his armies and strengthen his cavalry. In the end it would prove a mistake; if he had wanted, he could have negotiated a lasting peace instead of a temporary ceasefire. In the event, all the French roads leading towards the Rhine were soon thronged with new troops heading towards Saxony to join the rest of the army.

Spring 1813 had been successful for the French, and it looked as if this would continue as long their southern German allies supported this effort. Perhaps Napoleon's father-in-law, the Emperor of Austria, would join his side? Napoleon's intention was to separate the Russians and the Prussians from the English-organised coalition, and to impose his conditions on each of them.

Although he was pre-occupied by these strategic political questions, the rudimentary training received by the Guards of Honour had not escaped the emperor's attention. But he needed soldiers in Germany, and NCOs were more necessary in the field army than back home at the depots. His intention was to give them officers from within their own corps. The emperor was convinced that the Guards of Honour, kept under his own eye and close to his Imperial Guard, would learn their trade without delay. Until they could be promoted as officers for Line units, Napoleon would use them to manoeuvre in front of the enemy, practising their craft and making a useful show of force without being engaged in battle.

The deeper the first squadrons moved into Germany the closer they got to the emperor, and a first encounter could not be avoided for long. Informed that Napoleon was going to inspect his Guards of Honour, Gen. Dejean gave them time to adjust their uniforms and equipment and had them lined up in battle order. Napoleon arrived shortly afterwards; the soldiers dismounted and the emperor walked along their ranks, addressing himself to several of them. When he had done so, they remounted – and the emperor announced that he wished to see them manoeuvre.

General Dejean gave his orders; but if the presence of the emperor troubled the new recruits, it troubled their commanding officers even more – they knew that their troops were not well enough trained to execute their orders without difficulties. They had had to learn too much in too short a time. Even an order to execute a 'column by four to the right' or a 'turn back by four to the left' was enough to get them into a tangle. The marshals and generals of the staff who accompanied Napoleon, wishing to spare the emperor this unmilitary spectacle, came forward to guide the troops through the manoeuvres. They ended up as they had started, lined up in battle order.

Seeing that they were unequal to even the simplest of manoeuvres en masse, a senior officer thought that perhaps they might do better in grand manoeuvres by platoon, and the commander asked whether the emperor wished to see this. The Guards of Honour and their squadron officers knew better – they had never practised such movements. A foreign-born officer, new to the Guards of Honour (as were most of their officers) ordered them into motion. In spite of the shouted orders of the officers and the generals they ended up in total confusion. The emperor, with a glacial face, summoned the regimental officers and upbraided them for the lack of training; no one dared to point out to him that their soldiers had only been in the army for three months. He ordered them to train and exercise the soldiers without respite; more positively, he at last authorised the transfer into each company of a certain number of NCOs from the Old Guard, who arrived the next day.

A few days later Napoleon decreed that the 1st Regiment of Guards of Honour was to be attached to the Chasseurs à cheval of the Imperial Guard, the 2nd to the Grenadiers à cheval, the 3rd to the Dragoons, and the 4th to the 1st (Polish) Lancers of the Guard. They were subjected to the same discipline as the regiment to which they were attached, and were to follow them everywhere, in and out of battle. The commanders of the Old Guard cavalry regiments were responsible for their instruction; and in case of an alert, the Old Guard regiments were to

Job's well-known illustration of Guards of Honour in combat with Cossacks. As the Cossacks were the spearheads of the Allied army pushing westwards across Germany and into France, they frequently clashed with the French light cavalry; and since Napoleon relied increasingly on the strength and loyalty of the Imperial Guard, confrontations such as this must have been frequent. The officer leading the Guards (right), wearing a colpack, is followed by a trumpeter. (Collection of Belgian Royal Army Museum, Brussels)

send experienced men to guide the Guards of Honour into battle. Every day, each regiment would provide one captain, one sub-lieutenant, four sergeants, eight corporals and two trumpeters plus 80 troopers to serve with the duty squadrons of their affiliated Old Guard regiments which always accompanied the emperor.

On 15 September the Guards of Honour squadrons serving with the army formed part of the 3rd Imperial Guard Cavalry Division, commanded by Gen. Count Walther. The commander-in-chief of the entire Imperial Guard cavalry was Gen. Nansouty, who had his headquarters at Pirna. On that day the Guards of Honour mustered:

1st Regt: 13 officers, 45 officers' horses, 354 troopers, 367 troop horses
2nd Regt: 16 officers, 50 officers' horses, 286 troopers, 286 troop horses
3rd Regt: 7 officers, 20 officers' horses, 203 troopers, 211 troop horses
4th Regt: 6 officers, 24 officers' horses, 202 troopers, 202 troop horses.

One month later at Stötteritz, the figures were:

1st Regt: 15 officers, 50 officers' horses, 269 troopers, 265 troop horses
2nd Regt: 15 officers, 46 officers' horses, 246 troopers, 241 troop horses
3rd Regt: 8 officers, 24 officers' horses, 146 troopers, 147 troop horses
4th Regt: 10 officers, 34 officers' horses, 192 troopers, 184 troop horses.

The *Moniteur*, the official state newspaper, followed the advance and actions of the Guards of Honour. In the edition of 23 September 1813 it reported that on the heights of Peterswalde on 16 September, commanded by Gen. Ornano, the Guards of Honour were involved in chasing the enemy's cavalry into Bohemia. One day later, together with the Red (2nd, Dutch) Lancers of the Imperial Guard, they captured near Pirna two guns and a limber.

In the meantime the new squadrons, numbering from 6th upwards in each regiment, were marching off one by one from their depots towards Mainz, where they were ordered to exercise and to form a second line of defence between Hanau and Frankfurt.

Leipzig

It was at Leipzig that the Guards of Honour would experience their first real battle. Even at Dresden, on 26 and 27 August 1813, the squadrons that were present had been kept away from the fighting, some units serving only as skirmishers in co-operation with the regiments of the Imperial Guard to which they were linked. Casualties were low, and most guardsmen who had to leave the ranks did so because they were suffering from dysentery. Losses between August and October for all four regiments were mainly in horses, some 70 in all. The 1st and 2nd Regiments, with their companies mostly up to strength, had a total of five squadrons in the field – though some of the guardsmen received their instruction in the handling of the sword while actually waiting on the battlefield. The 5th Squadrons of the 1st and 2nd Regiments left Mainz on 1 October and

(continued on page 33)

Detail of an anonymous painting in gouache of the battle of Leipzig, showing Napoleon and his staff surrounded by his Imperial Guard. In the middle can be seen the Gardes d'honneur with drawn sabres. Leipzig would be their first major battle, where they were present without being seriously engaged. (Collection of Belgian Royal Army Museum, Brussels)

1: Gen. Count de Saint-Sulpice, Colonel, 4e Régiment
2: Gen. Count de Pully, Colonel, 1er Régiment
3: Gen. Count de Belmont-Briançon, Colonel-Major, 3e Régiment

A

1: Garde d'honneur, 2e Régiment, leaving The Hague
2: Garde d'honneur, 1er Régiment, full dress
3: Garde d'honneur, 1er Régiment

B

1: Officer, full dress
2: Officer, undress
3: Officer, barracks dress

C

1: Brigadier, 4e Régiment, full dress
2: Maréchal-des-logis, 3e Régiment, full dress
3: Garde d'honneur, escort dress

F. Courcelle

D

1: Trumpeter, as 1812 regulations
2: Trumpeter, 4e Régiment
3: Trumpeter, 1er Régiment

E

General Count de Ségur leading the 3e Régiment, Gardes d'honneur, at Rheims, 13 March 1814

F

1: Groom ('Tartar')
2: Trumpeter, 4e Régiment
3: Trumpeter, 2e Régiment

P. Courcelle

H

Gen. Dautancourt, in 1813 the colonel-major of the Polish Lancers, became responsible for the organisation and training of the Gardes d' honneur squadrons at Leipzig. Under pressure of events after the defection of the Saxon troops, he neglected Napoleon's order not to engage the new corps, and moved the squadrons into the gap in the French positions which the departure of the Saxons had created. (Collection of Belgian Royal Army Museum, Brussels)

marched towards Kassel, where they were united with the 5th Squadron of the 4th Regiment.

On 16 and 17 October 1813 the available squadrons of all four regiments, led by their respective Colonel-Majors de Pange, Mathan, de Saluces and Monteil, were united under the command of Col. Dautancourt – a major in the 1st (Polish) Lancers of the Imperial Guard – and followed Gen. Nansouty's Guard cavalry onto the field. Strengths were respectively 15 officers and 269 men (1st Regiment), 15 officers and 246 men (2nd), 8 officers and 146 men (3rd), and 10 officers and 192 men (4th), giving a total of 48 officers and 853 men, or 901 all ranks. Stationed in between the villages of Liebertwolkitz and Probstheide, Col. Dautancourt was given the order to manoeuvre with the Guards of Honour in such a way as to show the corps to the enemy but without exposing them too much. On the afternoon of the third day of the battle, 18 September, the Saxon troops from Gen. Reynier's VII Corps changed sides, creating a gap on Ney's left flank near the village of Paunsdorf. Colonel Dautancourt, who was then near Stötteritz and Molkau, also noticed the gap; he marched off with his Guards of Honour to cover the exposed sector, and sent a detachment of 50 men to scout in the direction of Ritschkebach. Two corporals of the 2nd Regiment, Hustin and Landry, rode with their platoon towards the Saxons, and shouted out to them to reconsider their act of treachery, but were received with gunfire. General Nansouty, seeing the Guards exposed and remembering Napoleon's orders, sent a message ordering them not to approach too close to the enemy. Colonel Dautancourt's move had attracted the enemy's attention, and their fire caused some losses. Corporal Landry of the 2nd Regiment stated that whole ranks were blown away by enemy cannon fire, and Guardsman Goethals had his horse shot under him and lost his baggage.

In the evening the Guards of Honour were withdrawn west of Leipzig. During the whole battle they had followed and backed up the cavalry of the Imperial Guard but, lacking experience, they had not been committed to take part in their charges. Officer casualties at Leipzig were Capt. Prince Galinelli, 1st Regiment, wounded; Lt. Urcedé, 2nd Regiment, killed; from the 3rd Regiment, Capts. Bertrand de Narcé and Bourlon de Chavanges and Lt. de la Brosse, wounded, and Lt. de Larroche mortally wounded; and Lt. Bachelet, 4th Regiment, wounded.

Hanau

In late October 1813 the Bavarians, pressed by the Allies to change sides, tried to cut off Napoleon's retreat towards France. After the battle of Leipzig the remains of the French army marched via Erfurt, Gotha and Fulda towards Mainz. To reach the latter town they had to go through the deep forest of Lamboy. In a clearing among its massive trees lay the small town of Hanau, outside which – believing that they faced an army retreating in utter disorder – there waited a combined Austro-Bavarian corps commanded by the Bavarian Count von Wrede. This force comprised some 33,000 infantry, 10,000 cavalry and about 100 cannon. In fact the French, though scattered and in a pitiful state, were retreating in good order, leaving many troops to garrison German cities as they withdrew.

On 30 October, still marching together with the cavalry of the Imperial Guard, the Guards of Honour had been travelling for several hours through the forest when they were informed that an enemy force was confronting the army. A cannonade began to be heard in the distance, and as they approached the scene of action they could hear shot crashing into the treetops, bringing heavy boughs tumbling down around them; flying splinters caused several casualties among the troops.

General Drouot posted 50 guns at the edge of the forest to blast a gap in the enemy lines and to silence their artillery. Noticing this danger, Von Wrede gave his Bavarian cavalry orders to charge the French battery. When the German troopers threatened to overrun the gun line, the Imperial Guard cavalry – to whom the Guards of Honour were still attached – received orders to come forward and engage the Bavarian cavalry. They charged through the woods up both sides of the road, leaving the roadway itself free for the army's wagons and guns. The charge saved Drouot's artillery by driving back the Bavarian cavalry, and within minutes the Guard cavalry had reached the by now abandoned enemy guns. In the meantime, Gen. Drouot's Imperial Guard artillery directed their fire over the cavalry's heads, this time driving back the enemy infantry with heavy casualties.

While the Imperial Guard charged with Line units from Gen. Sebastiani's 2nd Cavalry Corps, some 400 Guards of Honour of the 3rd Regiment advanced under the command of the officers de Saluces and d'Andlau. Arriving at the edge of the wood they found Gen. Exelmans, who indicated the direction they should take. Once formed up in battle array they advanced and charged, although their horses were by now exhausted. The Guards of Honour came to the relief of the Horse Grenadiers of the Imperial Guard, who were being driven back by the enemy; consequently this élite heavy regiment was able to regroup, and when the moment had passed 'the Gods' gave the 3rd Regiment a cheer of gratitude.

The battle was won by the early evening, and the troops were quartered near the town. The troopers had been without food for 24 hours, and hunger forced them into the houses in search of anything edible, though the only things they found were potatoes and apples stored in the cellars. After Hanau, Napoleon complimented his Guards of Honour for their service during the battle and a large number of crosses of the Legion of Honour were distributed. Expectations were high: with the experience the Guards had now acquired, which in turn had improved their morale and ésprit de corps, they could become crack troops within a few months.

The retreat towards France continued, however, and typhus raged through the ranks, killing more guardsmen than the enemy had laid low. Hospitals in and around Metz, Mainz – where some 20,000 French troops died – Erfurt and other cities were packed with victims. In the consequent confusion the army became disorganised, and some regiments fell apart. The exception was the Old Guard, which marched in one massive unit. The Guards of Honour who lost their horses during the retreat took cover among the ranks of the Old Guard infantry.

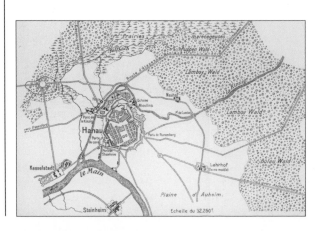

Map of Hanau, 1813. The Imperial Guard advanced on the town, under heavy artillery fire, along the upper of the two north-east roads through the Lamboy Wald, north of the River Kinzig.

In the 2nd Regiment of Guards of Honour, the company of volunteer Amand de Mendiéta, 113 strong at Leipzig, had only four men left when they returned to France. They were sent to Rambouillet, where they spent a couple of months in hospital to recover from the ordeal.

The Rhine

While the first-raised squadrons of the Guards of Honour crossed back over the Rhine after the battles of Leipzig and Hanau, the newly formed higher-numbered squadrons gathered around Mainz. (The exception was the 8th Squadron, 1st Regiment, which left Versailles on 30 November and was sent to Brussels – see below, 'The Belgian campaign'.) Marshal Kellermann, military commander of Mainz, received orders to send the newly arriving Guards of Honour into the Rhineland. In early September fresh troops of the 1st Regiment, commanded by Gen. Ricard, were at Worms and those of the 2nd, commanded by Col.Maj. de Pange, were at Spire.

Now the Guards of Honour were employed in the front lines. On 9 November 1813, still on the east bank of the Rhine, Capt. de Kerchove d'Exaerde, commander of an élite company of some 100 men of the 1st Regiment, was ordered by Marshal Macdonald to destroy the bridges across the Rhine and all other crossing points on the right bank. In December the captain was sent on reconnaissance towards Goettghen, Northeim and Braunschweig; always acting as vanguard, he took several prisoners whom he sent to Kassel. On 13 December the Russians attempted a night crossing of the Rhine between Mainz and Worms.

News of French reverses now came thick and fast, and word of the national uprising against the French in Holland caused a good deal of muttering among the guardsmen of Dutch origin, who began to desert – as did the Germans from the Lippe department. In due course orders were given to arrest and disarm the remaining Dutch guardsmen, who were to be conducted towards Landau by an armed escort. The Dutch, never very eager to serve, were more than once contacted by commissioners of the Provisional Government or of the Prince of Orange, encouraging them to change sides or simply to return home.

Nevertheless, despite the setbacks suffered by the French army, morale within the four regiments was generally good except for the Dutch, the Italians, and those recruited from the right bank of the Rhine. On 13 December Gen. Nansouty, after an inspection tour, wrote in his report to the emperor that the soldiers were generally badly clothed and equipped, badly led, and without good horses. The 4th Regiment was the worst, and the newly arrived squadrons of the 1st and 2nd (particularly the latter) were rather good. Again he appealed for proper officers, attaching to his report a list giving the names of Line officers who were available to pass into the regiments of Guards of Honour. Most of the officers who had served from the beginning did not know their job, and

Painting by J.Rouffet of the 3rd Regiment of Guards of Honour; he depicts them in full dress, with yellow-tipped plumes and red-edged shabraques, and the trumpeter (left) in dark green chevroned with the eagle-and-N 'Imperial livery' braid. Inexperienced as they were, the men of the new corps had to be instructed in their trade while marching to join the army in Germany. Serving under Napoleon's direct control, they would finally prove their qualities in their first major engagement on 30 October 1813 at Hanau, where 400 men of the 3rd Regiment charged with the Imperial Guard. After they had successfully intervened to support the outnumbered Grenadiers à cheval, 'the Gods' saluted them with shouts of *'Vive les Gardes d'Honneur!'* (Collection of Belgian Royal Army Museum, Brussels)

The winter of 1813–14 was extremely cold. The Dutch guardsman Van den Broecke drew this supply wagon, accompanied by a mounted officer protected against the cold by a cloak or voluminous cavalry overcoat. (Collection of Zeeuwse Bibliotheek, Holland)

several had already had to be sent home. Nevertheless, Nansouty added that most of the soldiers were in good spirits and eager to serve. With the necessary numbers of good NCOs and officers they could be made into fine regiments – as had been proved by the transfusion of Old Guard NCOs at Dresden.

Of the approximately 400,000 men with whom Napoleon set out to fight the 1813 German campaign, some 20,000 were killed at Leipzig; about 120,000 still remained in garrisons spread around Germany – including 25,000 in Hamburg, 20,000 in Dresden and 36,000 in Danzig – most of whom would surrender later that year. At the end of the campaign the emperor withdrew across the Rhine with only some 60,000 men; the rest were prisoners of war, deserters, or had died of typhus. In late 1813 and early 1814, Napoleon was forced to rebuild his army yet again.

One measure he chose was to strengthen his Old Guard cavalry regiments with numbers of Guards of Honour; 450 soldiers from each of the four regiments were to be transferred, of whom 200 were to join the existing Guard regiments and 250 the newly raised 1er Éclaireurs (1st Scouts) of the Guard. Colonel de Castellane complained that coming on top of the losses from casualties, desertion, disease, and the disarming of the Dutch, these new levies for the Imperial Guard would reduce the numbers to such an extent that the harmony between officers and men would be lost. On the other hand, some commanding officers saw an opportunity to get rid of their least capable and enthusiastic soldiers to the Guard depots.

New senior officers were also promoted to join the staffs of the regiments; due to the large establishments of the four units, their commanding officers had long been requesting them to ease the burdens of command. The 1st Regiment received Gen. Picquet as second-colonel; the 2nd, Gen. Vallin; the 3rd, Gen. Vincent, and the 4th Regiment, Gen. Merlin. General Lepic of the 2nd Regiment, suffering from his old head wounds, was replaced by Gen. de Langrange. These changes were decreed on 8 October 1813, by which date the regiments of Guards of Honour present with the army numbered:

1st Regt: 35 officers, 763 troopers, 867 horses
2nd Regt: 41 officers, 948 troopers, 1,134 horses
3rd Regt: 32 officers, 1,483 troopers, 1,374 horses
4th Regt: 63 officers, 1,820 troopers, 1,267 horses

Once again the colonels had to return to their depots to seek fit new recruits, and horseflesh, to fill the ranks.

THE CAMPAIGN OF FRANCE, 1814

During the night of 20/21 December 1813, Bernadotte's Allied army crossed the Rhine at six different places between Basle and Strasbourg, heading for the Netherlands some 60,000 strong. On 1 January 1814 it was the turn of Blücher's 75,000 Prussians, marching up the Moselle into Lorraine; and in the meantime the Austrian Schwarzenberg led 210,000 men into France via Switzerland. In the far south, Wellington's Anglo-Portuguese army was across the Pyrenees. The fundamental plan was simple: all the Allied armies would converge towards Paris. This massive push into France forced the thin and over-stretched French lines of defence to retreat and contract.

The remains of the 1st Guards of Honour, rallied by Maj. Chamboran, retreated through the Saarland to join Marshal Marmont's corps. Large parts of the 2nd Guards of Honour were forced to retire into besieged strongholds; the biggest element, commanded by Col. de Pange, formed part of the Mainz garrison and supported Gen. Morand's heroic defence of the town.

On 13 January 1814 the remainder of the four regiments were united into a cavalry division commanded by Gen. Defrance. Its two brigades were to be commanded by Gen. Picquet – with the 1st Guards of Honour and the 10th Hussars; and Gen. de Ségur – with the 2nd, 3rd and 4th Guards of Honour.

For the first time since the Revolution, the French now had to fight on their own territory. Instead of an army of several hundred thousand men, Napoleon had only some 118,000 west of the Rhine, a rag-bag scrambled together from conscripts and National Guardsmen around a core of veterans. Outnumbered on every side, they would march and counter march back and forth by day and night until they were stupid with fatigue. Troopers slept with their reins tied to their arms in case of an alert. Men and horses alike were exhausted and sick; the uniforms were worn and tattered, the horses needed reshoeing, and food

Travelling around Versailles, Paris and other cities, Van den Broecke noticed the departure of a military convoy guided by Gendarmes. (Collection of Zeeuwse Bibliotheek, Holland)

was running short. Nevertheless, Napoleon would lead them into the history books in one of his finest campaigns, and on occasions he came tantalisingly close to success.

On 20 January the 1st Regiment were at Verdun; on 10 February the Guards of Honour were at Champaubert; the next day they charged the Russians at Montmirail, and on the 12th they pursued the enemy towards Château-Thierry. On 25 February the Guards were with Marshal Mortier's corps at Meaux, and on 1 March they stood against Gen. Sacken's Prussians at Lizy-sur-Ourcq.

With the Russo-Prussian troops engaged against both the corps of Marshals Marmont and Mortier, Napoleon suddenly attacked Blücher's forces from the south, driving them towards the Aisne and Soissons. It would have been a total success if a general had not handed that city over – without a fight – to the retreating Prussians, thus allowing Blücher to escape from certain surrender.

Rheims, the last victory

Convinced of the need to destroy the Prussians before turning to face the advancing Austrians of the Army of Bohemia, Napoleon pressed on with the pursuit of the retreating Blücher. The Guards of Honour in Gen. Defrance's division formed part of Marshal Mortier's corps, and followed the enemy towards Braine and Oulchy-le-Château. On 6 March they were at Berry-au-Bac; the next day the Guards of Honour were engaged against the Russian cavalry of Gen. Winzingerode, and after a terrible night march, in snow and mist, they arrived in front of Laon.

Here, on the morning of 7 March 1814, Gen. Defrance received Mortier's order to march towards the threatened city of Rheims. When within sight of the city the Guards of Honour and the 10th Hussars found themselves facing a Russian cavalry force 1,000–1,200 strong, drawn up awaiting them in battle order. Defrance's division, though by now reduced to some 800 sabres, charged the Russians and drove them from the field, in an engagement which would be remembered as the battle of Coutures. The 1st Guards of Honour could field just 130 men; the

10th Hussars had some 500. The next day, Gen. Defrance and his division made their entry into Rheims, to be greeted by the citizens with gifts of wine and food.

In the meantime, a Russo-Prussian corps commanded by the émigré Gen. de Saint-Priest, which had taken part in the sieges of the now-surrendered cities of Torgau and Wittemberg, marched into France. General de Saint-Priest's one desire was to retake Rheims, which was now occupied by Gen. Corbineau with only a handful of men – Gen. Defrance's cavalry had left the city on 11 March. The next morning the latter learned that the enemy had retaken Rheims some two hours earlier. Gathering all available men, Gen. Defrance added some 500 infantry from the VI Corps and some 190 dragoons and cuirassiers under Gen. Bordesoulle to his division. With Rheims fallen once more, communications between the two major Allied armies were restored. Napoleon therefore ordered Marshal Marmont to march towards the city, and followed in person with the Imperial Guard.

General Defrance's division became the vanguard of the march towards Rheims, pushing enemy reconnaissance parties back towards the city and capturing two Prussian Landwehr infantry battalions. General de Saint-Priest, not expecting any serious French attempt to retake the city, had neglected defensive preparations on the various routes of approach. By the time he finally realised that he was under threat, his detachments patrolling the neighbourhood were already retreating into Rheims. Marmont, arriving in front of the city, halted to awaited the arrival of the emperor at around 4pm. The Russo-Prussian force made a sortie, but was quickly pushed back towards the city walls. At the same time the 3rd Guards of Honour and the small detachment of the 1st, led by Gen. de Ségur, charged the Russian dragoons who were concentrated at the Soissons–Epernay crossroads.

Count César Vachon de Belmont-Briançon, born in 1770, had served in the Gardes du Corps of the last King of France and as ADC to his father, who was a general. Emigrating during the Revolution and fighting against the regime, he nevertheless returned to France during Bonaparte's Consulate. Chamberlain to Napoleon in 1813, he became colonel-major of the 3rd Guards of Honour in June 1813 and took part in the campaigns of Saxony and France. He was shot on 13 March 1814 during the battle of Rheims, where he was buried in the North Cemetery. The officers of his regiment asked the famous painter Horace Vernet to paint this portrait representing him on the morning of the fatal day, wearing his campaign dress: tight-cut dark green trousers with silver buttoned side-stripes, a dark green pelisse with silver braid and sleeve rank stripes, and a red shako with one narrow and one wide rank stripes at the top and the white plume of a regimental staff officer. See Plate A3. (Collection of Belgian Royal Army Museum, Brussels)

Nothing could stop them, and the Russians who could not flee were killed or taken prisoner. The Guards' success was so great that they kept on pushing forward, passing beyond the other French troops; even two Russian infantry battalions who were mistaken for French troops were left unharmed behind them. Arriving in front of the city walls they charged a Russian artillery unit, sabring the gunners, killing the horses and capturing an enemy flag. But now, with the two Russian battalions behind them, they found themselves cut off from the rest of the army. Under fire from the city walls and under canister shot from two cannon, the Guards of Honour were also engaged by the infantry of Col. Skobeleff's Riazanski Regiment.

In the confusion a Belgian-born corporal by the name of Jean-François-Joseph-Alexandre de Steenhault, though serving in the 2nd Company, 1st Guards of Honour, found himself near the front of the 3rd Regiment's charge. Sabring everyone who opposed him, he was one of four men – including Gen. de Ségur – who entered the city first. Cut off from the rest of the Guards, who hesitated to pass through the narrow gateway, they had to fight for their lives. De Ségur, engaged in unequal combat against several dragoons, saw Cpl. François Daguerre and shouted, *'À moi, Brigadier!'* Daguerre went to his aid; then Cpl. de Steenhault joined him with some other guardsmen, and protected their wounded commander by standing around him and covering him with their bodies.

De Steenhault, with 14 wounds of which two appeared fatal, was left for dead as the fighting swirled on. After the battle he was found still breathing and taken to an ambulance, where he recovered. He was mentioned in Gen. Defrance's report, and admitted to the Legion of Honour on 14 March 1814. He would die in 1843, after a long career as mayor of Mechelen (Malines). His fellow countryman Sgt. Antoine Dhanis of the 1st Regiment also received the cross of the Legion of Honour for his conduct in charging the enemy's artillery; in 1830 he would become mayor of Antwerp.

General de Ségur would recover from his wounds, but those of Col.Maj. de Belmont-Briançon of the 3rd Regiment were mortal, in spite of the courage of Sgt. Fresneau who fought shoulder to shoulder with him. Among the wounded of the 3rd Guards of Honour one also finds Capt. Legoux du Plessis (mortally), Lts. de Kergrist, Martin de Bourgon and Sapinaud, and Sgt. Drouault – who suffered some 11 bayonet wounds, had his horse killed under him, and was taken prisoner. Casualties in the 1st Regiment included Lt. de Campigneulle, killed, and Lts. de la Génevraye, de La Londe, Périer, de Chambeau and Surgeon-

Rheims, 13 March 1814: Gen. de Ségur, charging at the head of his 3rd Regiment and part of the 1st (centre), was engaged in an unequal fight against several Russian dragoons. Wounded and outnumbered, he shouted to Cpl. François Daguerre of the 1st; the corporal stormed to his help, running down a Russian dragoon and disengaging his commander. Painting by Dupray; cf Plates F & G. (Collection of Belgian Royal Army Museum, Brussels)

Sgt. Antoine Dhanis, a native of Antwerp, charged the enemy artillery at Rheims with the small element of the 1st Regiment which was present; he had his horse killed under him, and received the cross of the Legion of Honour for his actions during the battle. In this rather dim but interesting painting he is portrayed in winter dress, wearing a closed pelisse on which we can see his cross. His shako plate has the cut-out regimental number; the tassels and flounders hanging down from his left shoulder are presumably from his shako retention cord. The buttoned leather cover to protect his shoulder belt is an item normally associated with officers. (Collection of Belgian Royal Army Museum, Brussels)

Major Thillaye, wounded. Even Gen. Picquet was wounded by a lance thrust while trying to help a guardsman who was beset by several Cossacks. In the ranks of the 1st Regiment, 24 guardsmen were killed and 13 wounded, 12 officers and 24 guardsmen were dismounted, and 23 others were 'lost'; in total 50 horses were killed. The papers of Sgt. Dhanis state that in the campaign as a whole his company lost 130 casualties from 250 men, but it is unclear exactly to what period he refers. Many men of the division were rewarded with the cross of the Legion of Honour and a promotion into the cavalry of the Imperial Guard, though this transfer was sometimes refused by the Guards of Honour.

Late in the evening the French army entered the city; but Rheims would be Napoleon's last victory. The lines of communication between the Allied armies had been cut once more, but weight of numbers would force the French army further and further back. On 17 March, Gen. Defrance's Guards of Honour Division was sent to join Marshal Ney's corps marching from the Marne towards the Aube, to support Marshal Macdonald's manoeuvres against the Austrians. The next day they were engaged near Arcis-sur-Aube against the lancers of Gen. Frimont, in a battle that would last until 20 March.

From the 10,000 Guards of Honour, only some 700 were still following Gen. Defrance (though we must recall that since the levies of December 1813 nearly another 2,000 of them had been serving in the cavalry regiments of the Imperial Guard). One squadron of the 1st Regiment was still operating in Belgium; the larger part of the 2nd Regiment was serving in the garrisons of besieged towns; and others were still at the regimental depots – like the 700 men, ready to march, who were kept inactive at Versailles.

The eastern garrisons

When the Allies crossed the Rhine to open the Campaign of France at the turn of 1813/14, the Guards of Honour had to abandon without delay their positions along the Rhine to join the corps of Marmont and Victor near Strasburg and Colmar. The 1st Regiment, cut off from the rest of the French army, succeeded in joining Marshal Marmont, while the 3rd and 4th joined Marshal Victor. During this retreat the 2nd Squadron, 3rd Regiment, commanded by Capt. Fournier de Bellevue, sought shelter in Landau on 2 January 1814. The 4th Regiment had a detachment trapped in Strasburg. General Choisy and nearly the whole of the 2nd Regiment – plus some 1,000 infantry of the 2nd Bde of Gen. Durutte's division, who had occupied Bingen to keep an eye on the River Nahe – marched into Mainz, and formed part of the garrison during the subsequent siege.

In Landau the squadron from the 3rd Regiment suffered only light casualties. Among the officers, Lt. Bournier was wounded on 26 February; during a sortie on 26 March, Lt. Provost de Saulty suffered a bullet wound and a lance thrust; on 9 April, the squadron commander, Capt. Fournier de Bellevue, was wounded. Casualties in the ranks during the siege, from 21 January until 26 March, were Sgt. Frotté de Maisonneuve, Cpl. Evesque, and Guardsman la Porte (who volunteered to serve as a foot skirmisher and was wounded by a bayonet thrust). Early in May the squadron left Landau with a strength of 141 men.

In Strasburg, on 24 January, 225 officers and men of the 4th Regiment took part in a sortie commanded by Col. Thurot of the 8th Hussars – who held overall command of the cavalry in the besieged town – and earned his praise in his after-action report. Kept as a reserve, they received the charging enemy cavalry with unshaken determination, forcing them to retreat. Major de Brouville was also praised for keeping his young and inexperienced soldiers under control. At the end of the day the Guards of Honour casualties were limited to two wounded horses. On 4 February the Guards of Honour again took part in a sortie, and again served with distinction. On 13 February the French troops made a sortie towards Robertsau; a detachment of Guards of Honour rode as vanguard, and mauled a post of Baden Landwehr soldiers near Buckel. Sergeants Marietti and Mounot were wounded (the regiment's only casualties), while Lt. Delamer was complimented for his conduct. On 10 March, at around 3pm, there was a small skirmish between eight Guards of Honour and some 60 Baden soldiers near the church of Robertsau; the guardsmen took two prisoners and had two horses wounded; Sgt. Valaux and Guardsmen Casset and Argillier were cited for their bravery. On 8 April, near Kehl, the Strasburg garrison made a sortie; the whole cavalry under command of Col. Thurot participated, and the Guards of Honour distinguished themselves once more. On 15 April, with an armistice signed and the siege over, the detachment of the 4th Regiment of Guards of Honour had a strength of 26 officers and 391 men with 353 horses.

The bulk of the 2nd Guards of Honour, under Gen. de Pange and reinforced by some hundred guardsmen from the 1st Regiment, were trapped in Mainz for nearly three months. Typhus raged through the garrison, and few who entered hospital came out alive. Alerts were frequent, as were sorties; on 4 February, Capt. Nicod of the 2nd was wounded. General Morand successfully held the city to the end, only surrendering his 12,000-odd men on 4 May, nearly a month after the capitulation of Paris. The four first squadrons of the 2nd Guards of Honour numbered, on 26 April 1814, 39 officers and 441 men with 567 horses.

The Belgian campaign

The threats to Napoleon's dwindling empire did not come only from the east and south, however, but also from the north, where Gen. Maison tried to check an Allied push towards Antwerp. The 8th Squadron (15th & 16th Cos), 1st Regiment of Guards of Honour, commanded by Capt. Count de Saint-Paër, left for Belgium on 30 November and arrived at Mechelen (Malines) on 30 January 1814. On 11 January the French near Antwerp had been forced to retreat – under pressure from English, Prussian and Russian troops – from their line of defence between Brasschaat, Hoogstraten and Turnhout. Four days later they had to evacuate Deurne and Merksem, two villages close to Antwerp. The squadron of Guards of Honour was split into several detachments; one of them – nine officers with 204 troopers and 221 horses, commanded by Capt. Count de Saint-Paër – served under Gen. Lazare Carnot in the besieged port of Antwerp, holding out until the Restoration. The others served in Gen. Castex's reduced cavalry corps of Gen. Maison's I Corps, marching from one place to the other, trying to keep the north of France and Flanders free from the Allies. On 30 March, marching from Ghent towards Kortrijk, the Guards of Honour and a detachment of Chasseurs à cheval of the Young Guard made a successful charge on enemy troops at Courtrai. It would be the last action on this front; the following day the Allies entered Paris, and on 11 April, Napoleon formally abdicated.

The Restoration

On 1 April 1814, Gen. Defrance gathered his division near Saint-Germain; on that date his Guards of Honour could muster a combined strength equivalent to just one weak squadron:

1st Regt: 9 officers and 26 troopers with 56 horses
2nd Regt: 14 officers and 76 troopers with 101 horses
4th Regt: 12 officers and 80 troopers with 110 horses

From Saint-Germain they marched towards Pithiviers, where they were joined by several detachments. On 10 April the Dutch guardsmen who had been kept under surveillance were released and sent home. Rumours of Napoleon's abdication proved true. Unwilling as some of them had been to serve Bonaparte when they were originally called up, the abdication was not generally greeted with enthusiasm in the ranks. The time they had passed in the army and on campaign had naturally created a real ésprit de corps, and a respect for the way Napoleon had sought to defend France.

The scattered troops returning to France were often inspected by members of the restored Bourbon royal family. The 1st Regiment of the Guards of Honour was inspected by the Duc de Berry, and Gen. de Pully had to send a detachment to escort the king to Paris; two squadrons were formed and marched in the vanguard of King Louis' escort. Ordered to shout 'Long live the King!', the first platoon obeyed – but the tail of the escort shouted 'Long live the Emperor!'

The Royal Ordnance of 24 June 1814 disbanded the four regiments of Guards of Honour. General Exelmans dissolved the 1st Regiment at Versailles on 14 July; the next day it was the turn of the 4th Regiment; on 17 July the 3rd Regiment was disbanded at Tours, and on the 22nd, the 2nd Regiment at Rambouillet.

However, the king did keep one of Napoleon's promises: some 900 of the remaining French Guards of Honour entered the companies of the Gardes du Corps of King Louis XVIII, and all of them were breveted sub-lieutenant. The other guardsmen returned to their homes in Italy, Holland, Germany, Switzerland and Belgium.

When Napoleon returned from Elba in 1815 and marched towards Paris, some former Guards of Honour joined the column; later 87 of them would ask permission to serve in the Imperial armies.

Conclusion: some misconceptions

The Guards of Honour were never an official part of the Imperial Guard, but their exact status was and remains the subject of confusion.

OPPOSITE **Rheims is packed with Napoleonic monuments, several of them in the city's North Cemetery. One, raised in 1893 in commemoration of the battle, has on its four sides the following legends: 'In memory of Prince Gagarine, commander of the Baschkirs, killed at the Paris Gate on 5 March 1814, aged 23; of Joseph de Heck, captain of the Russian Staff, knight of the Orders of Saint Anne and Vladimir, born in 1785, killed at the battle of the Promenades on 19 March 1814.** *Inter Arma Caritus*. **On the right side: 'In memory of the French soldiers killed in the defence of Rheims in 1814.** *Pro Patria Ceciderunt. Le Souvenir Français*. **On the left side: 'To the Russian soldiers killed at Rheims in 1814.** *Hostes … Fratres …*'. **Above this we find one in memory of a Guard of Honour: 'César-René Marie François Rodolphe de Vachon, Count de Belmont Briançon, Colonel-Major of the 3rd Regiment Guards of Honour, married to Mlle Clémentine de Choiseul-Gouffier, killed at the defence of Rheims on 13 March 1814.** *Decorum Pro Patria Mori*. **De Belmont-Briançon's remains do not lie under this monument; his original grave had as epitaph: 'Here rests the body of M. Count de Briançon de Belmont [sic], Colonel-Major of the 3rd Regiment of Guards of Honour, aged 50, killed at the battle of Rheims, on 13 March 1814'. (Alain Chappet Collection, France)**

Their undress uniforms resembled those of the Chasseurs à cheval of the Imperial Guard; they earned the same pay as that crack regiment; the four regiments served in the field in close association with the cavalry of the Guard; and most of the soldiers and officers considered themselves as being part of it. This resulted in confusion between the Ministry of War and the commanding officers of the four regiments. One of the proofs that they considered themselves Guard regiments was the introduction of sky-blue uniforms for their trumpeters, instead of the green worn by Line regiments (it should also be noted that the tunes they played were those used by the Guard trumpeters).

As already mentioned, not all the soldiers in the Guards of Honour were from rich families. A number were poor boys who had been paid to take the place of someone who could afford to buy a replacement. It is also clear that the definition of the 'leading' social classes, from which the regiments were supposed to be recruited, was in fact elastic enough to admit many from *arriviste* families whose pretensions outstripped their resources.

While in 1813 a large number of guardsmen felt themselves to be more or less 'hostages', regarded with some suspicion for their royalist or foreign backgrounds, in 1814 they felt that they had played an honourable role in history. They had participated in famous battles, serving under renowned generals alongside the Imperial Guard, 'the élite of the élite'. Moreover, they had served under the eyes of Napoleon himself, who had shown a real interest in them.

Later, when Napoleon III was on the throne, he instituted the Médaille de Sainte-Hélène, a medal for all the veterans of the Revolutionary and Imperial Wars. With all the actual miseries forgotten, and remembering only the good times and glorious moments, a number of French, Belgian, German, Italian, Swiss or Dutch former Guards of Honour applied for the medal. Even in Holland, more than one of whose guardsmen had spent much of their service thinking more about desertion than fighting for Napoleon's cause, they gathered on Thursday 18 June 1863. (The date to commemorate their service in the Guards of Honour was strangely chosen, as it also fell on the day that the battle of Waterloo had been fought, 48 years earlier.) Fifty years after their incorporation, former Guard of Honour Hoffman – once secretary to Col.Maj. de Pange and a lieutenant in the 2nd Regiment, and now a wealthy merchant and politician from Rotterdam – invited all surviving Dutch members of his former regiment to a commemorative dinner. From the 300 Dutchmen who had served in the regiment, only 47 could be traced in addition to the host; in the end a total of 25 veterans attended. Later, in December of that year, one of the participants had a bronze medal struck to commemorate the reunion dinner, bearing the names of all those who had taken part.

SELECT BIBLIOGRAPHY

Archives in the library of the Belgian Royal Army Museum, Brussels

Carnet de la Fourragère, Belgium, various issues (1924–65)

La Sabretache, France, various issues

Dr Lomier, *Histoire des Régiments de Gardes d'Honneur 1813–1814* (Amiens/Paris, 1924)

Dr W.F.Lichtenauer, *De Nederlanders in Napoleons Garde d'Honneur* (Rotterdam/The Hague, 1971)

F.H.N.Bloemink, *De lotgevallen van een Garde d'Honneur* (Gouda, 1913)

H.Lachouque, *La Garde Impériale*, Lavauzelle (1982)

J.Tranié & J.C.Carmigniani, *Napoléon 1814, La Campagne de France* (Paris, 1989)

L.Fallou, *La Garde Impériale 1804–1815* (Paris, 1901)

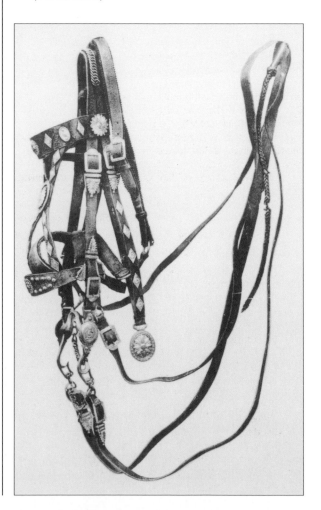

THE PLATES

A1: General Count de Saint-Sulpice, Colonel, 4e Régiment

After Rigo. As a *général de division* he is shown in full dress, wearing a colpack (busby) instead of the shako. Rank distinctions include not only the standard three silver stars of this grade of general officer, but also gold lace on the front of his riding breeches. Normally officers of his rank wore six rows of lace, but Bonardi de Saint-Sulpice, as a former general of the Imperial Guard and Colonel of the Dragoons of the Guard, still wears Guard rank distinctions – eight rows of lace, to which three stars are added on the forearms.

A2: General Count de Pully, Colonel, 1er Régiment

The four commanding officers of the Gardes d'honneur – like most regimental colonels of the Imperial Guard – considered their regiments as to some extent their own property. *Général de division* de Pully, as colonel of the 1st Regiment, is seen dressed in a regimental uniform rather than that prescribed for general officers. It is of fine quality materials and tailoring, with the gold lace and cording of superior officers instead of the normal silver, with the three stars of his general's rank added to the shako flounders and those of the security cord, and to the embroidery of the sleeves. The red trousers lack the hussar-style thigh embroidery that one would normally expect, but the outside seams are embellished with a wide double gold stripe with extra gold lace tracery along the sides. An imitation pantherskin shabraque edged in gold and green completed this officer's striking and luxurious appearance.

A3: General Count de Belmont-Briançon, Colonel-Major, 3e Régiment

As colonel-major (second-in-command) of the regiment he is depicted in his posthumous portrait by Vernet in the campaign dress which he was presumably wearing when he was mortally wounded at Rheims. This uniform shows, in contrast with the first two, a tendency towards more practical dress when in the field. All lace and cording is silver, indicating that gold was the prerogative of the commanding officers only – cf A1 and A2. Count de Belmont-Briançon wears long dark green trousers with silver buttons and stripes down the outer seams.

B1: Garde d'honneur, 2e Régiment, on departure from The Hague

During their brief existence the four regiments of Guards of Honour never received regimental standards. The tricolour flag depicted here is an example of those presented by some of the departments to the different detachments leaving to join their garrisons. For the Departement des Bouches de la Meuse the prefect's wife, Mme. de Stassart, embroidered a flag for every detachment. Volunteer Masschek carried the flag of the first detachment, but when he saw it the irascible Gen. Lepic had it taken away and destroyed. One embroidered flag from the same department still survives in the collection of the Rijksmuseum in Amsterdam.

Light cavalry bridle and reins as used by the Guards of Honour. (Author's collection)

Jacques Thomas de Pange (1770–1850). Son of the second Marquis de Pange, he was a royalist to his backbone. As a captain in the Berchény Hussars he served at the Tuileries to protect the royal family against the Revolution, and later emigrated and fought to avenge them. He returned to Napoleonic France; was named as Chamberlain to Napoleon and Count of the Empire in 1810; and was at the head of the local Guard of Honour when the emperor visited Metz. With France under threat of invasion he offered his sword to the emperor and became colonel-major of the 2nd Regiment. De Pange was much loved by his soldiers, and was one of the few senior officers who actually fought with his regiment. A liberal by persuasion, he would serve all French governments until his death. He is shown here in a double-breasted riding coat with crossed lapels and aiguillettes; see Plate C3. (Collection of Belgian Royal Army Museum, Brussels)

B2: Garde d'honneur, 1er Régiment, in full dress
After Martinet. The Gardes d'honneurs were uniformed like hussars. The differences between the four regiments were limited to little more than the tip of the dark green shako plume, one-fifth of the total length: red for the 1st Regiment, sky blue for the 2nd, yellow for the 3rd and white for the 4th. The regimental number was displayed on the shako plate and sabretache, showing here an eagle without imperial crown and with its head turned to the left as viewed, instead of to the right as was more common. The sabre illustrated has no sword knot but shows an eagle head on the pommel. Martinet did not represent the white cloth regimental number on the portmanteau. The same hand-coloured engraving

was used for all four regiments, with only the colour of the plume and the numbers changed. Given that a large number of the guardsmen had some financial means, they would have followed the latest fashions as they were wont to do in civilian life. When Martinet published his print light green gloves were in vogue, as we see here.

B3: Garde d'honneur, 1er Régiment
After A.van den Broecke. In his memoirs Guardsman van den Broecke includes two fine drawings showing soldiers of his regiment, which are reproduced on pages 8 and 10 of this book. Each wears a pelisse edged with white fleece instead of the usual black fur. One pelisse in the Army Museum at Brussels shows dark brown fur. The sabretache depicted conforms to the regulations.

C1: Officer in full dress
The uniforms of the officers were in the same style as those of their troopers except that all white cords, lace and white metal became silver or silver-plated. Officers might also sometimes choose to wear a fur colpack instead of the shako.

C2: Officer in undress uniform
As well as the hussar-style uniform, the Guards of Honour were ordered to obtain an undress uniform in the style of the Chasseurs à cheval of the Guard: a dark green *habit* with scarlet collar and cuffs, Hungarian-style breeches, and a silver-braided waistcoat. Even though not officially considered as Imperial Guard units, they were allowed to wear that organisation's distinctive aiguillettes. This order of dress was completed with a black bicorn with tassels at front and back and a tricolour cockade fastened by a loop and button. The difference between troopers and officers was the same as for the hussar-style uniform – white lace and embellishments for the enlisted ranks and silver for the officers.

C3: Officer in barracks dress
A portrait (left) of Col.Maj. Count de Pange, 2nd Regiment, shows him wearing a light undress coat or *'redingote'*. An unusual feature is the folded-back, round-topped lapels, conforming to the round lapels of some light cavalry undress uniforms. The coat was dark green, with a scarlet lining revealed by crossing the lapels. This uniform would have been worn at the depot garrison or when off duty. A fatigue cap might also be worn, of the general pattern, with a dark green turban braided silver round the edge, and a dark green wing piped in scarlet and tipped with a silver tassel.

D1: Brigadier, 4e Régiment, full dress
D2: Maréchal-des-logis, 3e Régiment, full dress
The uniforms of NCOs did not differ much from those of the troopers. The corporal of the 4th Regiment – note rank insignia above the cuff – is taken from a contemporary miniature (see page 46), and displays the typical appearance of a fashionable young man of the bourgeois class. The sergeant of the 3rd is reconstructed from surviving items in the Brunon Collection; note that all lace and cording on his uniform is in mixed dark green and silver. The scarlet shako has a shako cord and tassels in the same style. The top band of the shako was laced in silver; the shako plate and chin scales were silver-plated.

D3: Garde d'honneur in escort dress, Leipzig
At the Bibliothèque Marmottan in Paris is a contemporary gouache showing Napoleon and his staff at a battle somewhere in Germany in 1813. Behind a line of what can be considered as Gendarmes d'Élite may be seen a

detachment of Guards of Honour, with trumpeters and commanding officer, escorting the emperor; we know that every day two officers, two trumpeters and 92 NCOs and troopers were ordered to turn out with the Guard cavalry duty squadron. The troopers wear the regulation uniform; however, the dark green shabraques are of the light cavalry style, replacing the white sheepskin regimental pattern. Was this a 'free interpretation' by the artist, or an accurate detail? We know that all equipment was scarce at the start of the 1813 campaign and that what was available had to be shared between cavalry units. Contemporary paintings like these will always keep their enigmas.

E1: Trumpeter, conforming with 1812 regulations

To standardise the uniforms of drummers and trumpeters throughout the army, in place of the wide range of regimental 'fantasies' which had previously flourished, Napoleon decreed new dress regulations under which all were to wear the 'Imperial Livery'. For this branch of the cavalry the livery consisted of a green dolman and pelisse, with seven bands of lace on the sleeves and the same lace edging the collar and cuffs. The lace was yellow or alternating yellow and green, with red edges, black divisions, and green or green and yellow details – an Imperial eagle motif and a crowned 'N' alternating on contrasting backgrounds.

E2: Trumpeter, 4e Régiment

The number of the regiment is conjectural, but acceptable after original sources. This figure is after the gouache in the Bibliothèque Marmottan (see D3), where it is surprising to see that the trumpeters are dressed in red. The dolman is in fact in reversed colours, as was more or less traditional in the French cavalry; the pelisse is as for the troopers but trimmed with white sheepskin. The yellow pompon on the shako is

Constantin Charles Vanhavre (1794–1855). This important miniature shows clearly the full dress of a corporal in the 4th Regiment; cf Plate D2. The top band of his shako seems to be of interlaced silver rings, as was the fashion in the late Empire. His shoulder belt is of a different colour than the standard white leather. Note, too, the Austrian knot breeches decoration, a variation seen in a number of pictorial sources including a drawing – presumably from life – by Guardsman van den Broecke. (Author's collection)

LEFT Officers had the right to wear colpacks, but most of them followed the current fashion in military uniforms and went for the shako – some of them of the very latest fashion, the 'stovepipe' *shako rouleau*. This is a more conventional example. Shakos were made in hard cardboard or cow's leather covered with red cloth. Most of the officers ordered and paid for their own shakos, producing many differences between the surviving officers' examples. Here the shield of the shako plate beneath the Imperial Eagle shows the words 'GARDE' in a straight line above 'D'HONNEUR' in an arc, instead of the more usual regimental number. As in the portrait of Sgt. Dhanis on page 40, the tassels and flounders may have been unusual for this late in the Empire. (Author's collection) surprising for this regiment but is taken from the original painting; equally surprising are the yellow metal plate and chin scales. Another trumpeter in the picture wears the same dress but a black shako – at present the difference is unexplained.

E3: Trumpeter, 1er Régiment
Reconstruction after sources from Bucquoy. This trumpeter is in campaign dress, with Imperial Guard-style pale blue dolman, regimental *charivari* worn over the boots, and a red pompon in place of the tall full dress shako plume. Original text sources give full dress red breeches with lace decoration in white mixed with light blue; we have no information about the design or arrangement of this special feature.

F & G: General Count de Ségur leading the 3e Régiment, Gardes d'honneur at Rheims, 13 March 1814
At about 4pm on the afternoon of 13 March, Gen. de Ségur (right background) commanding the second brigade of Gen. Defrance's cavalry division, and regimental colonel of the 3rd Regiment of Guards of Honour – charged a Russian battery at the head of his regiment. Followed by the trumpet-major to pass his orders, he overran the Russian artillery and the Rizianski infantry regiment that covered it. This success took Gen. de Ségur into the narrow streets of Rheims, accompanied at first by only three men and later by some 60 of his guardsmen. Cut off, surrounded and under enemy fire, the party suffered high casualties, and de Ségur only narrowly escaped certain death thanks to the loyalty of his men.

The 1814 campaign was fought during winter, and the Guards of Honour wore their usual campaign dress with covered shako, overalls, and the pelisse as an extra jacket against the bitter cold; only the yellow pompon identifies the 3rd Regiment. The rolled-up coat was often worn over the shoulder to give some protection against sabre cuts and bullets. In the right foreground is a major, identified by the alternating gold and silver lace of this rank on both his uniform and shabraque.

H1: Groom ('Tartar')
Most of the volunteers for the Guards of Honour were eager to show good conduct on the battlefield; but the menial tasks, such as stable duties, were not quite what the young gentlemen had had in mind when they contemplated military glory. Some brought personal servants with them to their depots, and soon after the formation of the regiments Napoleon agreed to allow one groom to deal with stable duties for every two guardsmen. Mounted and armed with a pistol and light cavalry sabre, these 'tartares' could also be employed in the field – when commanding officers thought fit – as skirmishers or scouts for the regiments, although no real proof exists that this was ever actually tried. Regulations specified this simple uniform with black shako, grey tunic and trousers faced and trimmed with dark green, and light cavalry boots.

H2: Trumpeter, 4e Régiment
After Knötel. Serving with the Imperial Guard, the Guards of Honour had a status that was so ill-defined that even the commanding officers asked whether or not they were Guard units. Some of them clad their trumpeters in sky blue, a colour mainly used by Guard cavalry trumpeters. This man wears full dress: a sky blue pelisse with black fur trim and white cording and lace, a sky blue dolman with scarlet collar

Guard of Honour François-Joseph Dutilleux, born at Namur in Belgium; he was 1.66m (5ft 5ins) tall when he entered the corps as a volunteer, leaving his department on 19 July 1813 to serve in the 2nd Regiment. This portrait shows the dandyism prevalent among the wealthier members of the Guards of Honour; his shako is worn tilted to one side, and a tall white shirt collar emerges above the edge of the dolman collar. (Collection of Belgian Royal Army Museum, Brussels)

and cuffs and white cording and lace. Like some officers, trumpeters also wore black busbies with a scarlet bag trimmed in white and a green plume with a regimentally coloured tip – here, white.

Trumpeters rode grey horses; note his distinctive black sheepskin shabraque – instead of the troopers' white – edged with dark green 'wolves' teeth'. In full dress and for parades the trumpets were fitted with banners in green edged and fringed with gold lace and bearing a gold embroidered crowned Imperial eagle.

H3: Trumpeter, 2e Régiment
This trumpeter wears campaign dress consisting of a sky blue dolman faced in red with white lace and braid, and red campaign overalls reinforced with black leather and embellished with a sky blue stripe on the outer seams. His shako is protected with a black waxed cloth cover showing a sky blue pompon indicating the regiment.

INDEX

Figures in **bold** refer to illustrations

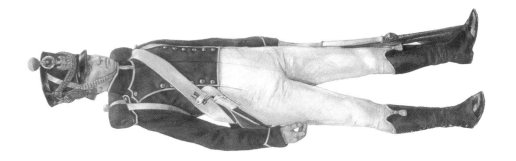

OSPREY
PUBLISHING

FIND OUT MORE ABOUT OSPREY

❏ Please send me the latest listing of Osprey's publications

❏ I would like to subscribe to Osprey's e-mail newsletter

Title/rank

Name

Address

Postcode/zip   state/country

e-mail

I am interested in:

❏ Ancient world
❏ Medieval world
❏ 16th century
❏ 17th century
❏ 18th century
❏ Napoleonic
❏ 19th century

❏ American Civil War
❏ World War I
❏ World War II
❏ Modern warfare
❏ Military aviation
❏ Naval warfare

Please send to:

USA & Canada:
Osprey Direct USA, c/o MBI Publishing, P.O. Box 1,
729 Prospect Avenue, Osceola, WI 54020

UK, Europe and rest of world:
Osprey Direct UK, P.O. Box 140, Wellingborough,
Northants, NN8 2FA, United Kingdom

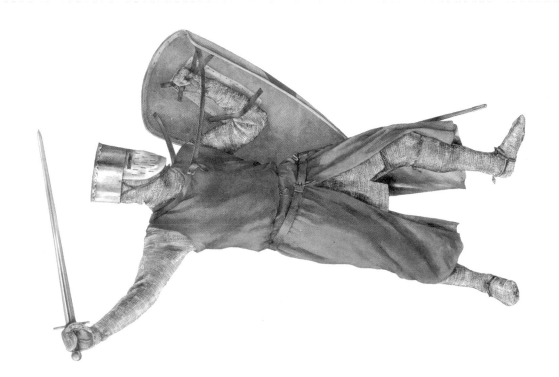

OSPREY
PUBLISHING

www.ospreypublishing.com

call our telephone hotline
for a free information pack

USA & Canada: 1-800-826-6600
UK, Europe and rest of world call:
+44 (0) 1933 443 863

Young Guardsman
Figure taken from *Warrior 22:*
Imperial Guardsman 1799–1815
Published by Osprey
Illustrated by Richard Hook

Knight, c.1190
Figure taken from *Warrior 1: Norman Knight 950 – 1204 AD*
Published by Osprey
Illustrated by Christa Hook

POSTCARD